THE WORLD OF NEGOTIATIONS:

Never Being a Loser

THE WORLD
OF
NEGOTIATIONS:
Never Being a Loser

Peter L. Grieco, Jr.
Paul G. Hine

PT Publications, Inc.
4360 North Lake Blvd.
Palm Beach Gardens, FL 33410
(407) 624-0455

Library of Congress Cataloging in Publication Data

Grieco, Jr., Peter L., 1942-
        The World of Negotiations: never being a loser / Peter L. Grieco
Jr., Paul G. Hine.

        Includes bibliographical references and index.
        ISBN 0-945456-06-9
        1. Negotiation in business. 2. Industrial procurement. I. Hine,
Paul G., 1953-   II. Title.
HD58.6.G74   1990
658.4--dc20   90-26684
                                                      CIP

Copyright © 1991 by PT Publications, Inc.

Printed in the United States of America.

TABLE OF CONTENTS

PREFACE

We wrote this book with the purpose of providing information which can be used, instead of providing stories and anecdotes about a negotiator's latest conquest. That requires interpretation by the reader. Not only does this style run counter to a win/win strategy, but we believe stories about another person's success are only valuable when they can be reinforced with solid and practical guidelines. Our book provides solid and practical tactics and strategies which can be used not only by purchasing professionals, but by each of us in our daily dealings, whether we are purchasing a home, a car or manufacturing components.

This book is designed to assist you or a company in devising, implementing and maintaining *a strategic plan for negotiation.*

Few, if any, of the existing books on negotiation focus on the methodology for how to deal with vendors, suppliers or third parties. No books provide details on the requirements for developing long-term, win/win agreements. Every company executive, manager and employee needs to know how to integrate proven methods of inventory management, quality control, supplier base management, process control, set-up reduction and so on as part of the negotiation process. Each and every one of these innovations in management philosophy is, in itself, a powerful negotiation tool. A customer, who uses these innovations and who understands their concepts and importance has significant negotiating clout.

We wanted this book to fill a void in the current literature available about negotiating in a World Class and global marketplace. Our book covers the development of a negotiating strategy based on Total Cost, not pricing; Total Quality Control, not inspection; Just-In-Time Delivery, not late delivery; Partnerships, not adversarial relationships.

Most of all, we wanted to write a book which stressed the importance and benefits of partnership. The goal of negotiating should be to develop a long-term, profitable relationship with suppliers and customers. We believe that a true partnership exists when there is a commitment by both parties to work side by side to solve problems. In addition, we think that there should also be a commitment to share profits which result from this effort. But how many people know how to negotiate this type of agreement? Too few, we are sad to say. Our book will illustrate how sellers can be encouraged to pursue cost reduction techniques, using win/win tactics, and avoid the old "hit them until they agree" method of negotiating.

Our explanations of negotiating strategies and tactics are reinforced by our real-life examples. Perhaps showing you how to negotiate in the world arena is the greatest strength of our book. Many of our trading partners already follow our doctrine. Here's hoping that you will enjoy success as you employ our ideas, techniques and examples.

Peter L. Grieco, Jr.
Paul G. Hine

West Palm Beach, FL

ACKNOWLEDGMENTS

In a very real sense, this book requires us to thank everybody who has taken our negotiation courses or contributed to all of the previous books in PT Publications' series on business excellence. Without these real-world experiences to build upon, we would have just written another academic book on negotiation. Thanks to all the suppliers and customers who were "tough" on us and taught us to sharpen our skills.

We would like to thank Gerry Price, Executive Vice President of Barr Laboratories, for reviewing our manuscript and offering his valuable insight. As always, we appreciate the assistance we get from our highly professional consulting group and our administrative staff.

Special thanks to Gerry Cunningham, of the MGI Management Institute, with whom we created the successful National Association of Purchasing Management (NAPM) home study course on negotiation. In addition, our thanks go to R. Jerry Baker, CPM, Executive Vice President of NAPM, for his support of our publicly-held negotiation programs sponsored by NAPM. They have greatly helped by providing us with actual case examples.

Much appreciation and thanks is also due to Kevin Grieco for his creative jacket and cover design and to Mark Grieco, whom I love dearly and who is the real negotiator of the family. We want to express also our continued appreciation to Steven Marks for his ability to put our ideas into the best possible editorial condition.

We know that this book will move us all toward the spirit of partnerships, rather than confrontation.

THE WORLD OF NEGOTIATIONS:

Never Being a Loser

negotiate (ni-go´-she-at) *v.* **-ated, -ating, -ates.** To discuss with a view to reaching agreement.

To My Family:

Leslie, Sarah, Lisa and Timmy
whom I thank for teaching me
that giving can be more joyous
than receiving.

Paul

To Mary who taught me
a valuable lesson:
The best things in life are free,
with or without negotiations.

Peter

CHAPTER ONE

*"Let us begin anew, remembering on both sides
that civility is not a sign of weakness, that sincerity is
always subject to proof. Let us never negotiate out of fear,
but let us never fear to negotiate."*

— John F. Kennedy

WIN/WIN: ESTABLISHING THE PARTNERSHIP

There isn't a person in the world who doesn't like to think of himself or herself as an ace negotiator, a real horse trader. Nobody wants the wool pulled over their eyes. Everybody would rather see themselves as able to go one-on-one with Donald Trump and come out with him saying, "He drove a hard bargain. I couldn't say no." Some of us would even like to outbargain the Devil himself for our soul! In short, when it comes to negotiating, we tend to see ourselves not as we really are, but as we would like to be. We slide over from real world to the world of fantasy, dreams and games. Just remember that when you're dreaming, your eyes are shut and it's fairly easy to pull the wool over your eyes. Dreams can be expensive. Tough negotiators may let you achieve your dreams (and theirs!) at your expense.

In the 1990s, we will find that negotiating doesn't have to be an either/or situation, that is, either I win or you lose. With training and planning, anybody can fashion and close deals which satisfy the needs and wants of all parties. Stop thinking of yourself as a horse trader who is going to foist an old nag on some country rube and start thinking of yourself as a negotiator. Negotiating has been, in many cases, an "I win/you lose" game. That attitude reminds me of when I was a kid playing out on the streets of my neighborhood with the big kids. One game that the big kids (they were probably twelve years old) would like to play is flipping pennies. They would flip and you would call "heads" or "tails." Now the rule was this, as put forth by the big kids: "Heads I win, tails you lose."

I remember the first time I heard that. It sounded reasonable. Well, it only took a couple of flips for me to realize what was going on. You can't fool a six-year-old for too long. I was never going to win if I accepted the big kids' terms and conditions. Of course, in my neighborhood, I was never going to change those terms and conditions either. Instead of presenting the big kids with a more fair alternative, I just stopped doing business with them. I found some three-year-olds down the street ...

Just kidding. I didn't look for somebody else to trick, but I did learn that a game wasn't very fun if you could only lose.

NEGOTIATION IN THE NEWS

For years, the countries of Eastern Europe had a deal with the Soviet Union where they couldn't win. The deal was this: Start a revolution in Hungary in 1956, the Soviets send in Russian tanks. Start a revolution in Prague in 1968, the Soviets send in Russian tanks. Try to start a labor union in Poland, the Soviets send in advisors. It wasn't until the Soviets learned that they were losing by "winning" all the time that the real or implied threat of tanks was removed from their negotiating strategy. Mikhail Gorbachev realized that all these tanks meant less bread on the Russian table. And that there weren't enough tanks to use as a negotiating tactic to keep both Eastern Europe and the Russian people in balance.

The Soviet Union's "heads I win, tails you lose" strategy worked for over forty years, but look at how quickly it appears to be coming unglued. It certainly didn't foster a long-term relationship. As the Soviet empire is dismantled, Russia may, as time will tell, be left with no partners it can trust or who can trust it. Here's a perfect example of how a "Soviet" strategy of negotiating may have short-term benefits, but invariably becomes a long-term disaster.

Whether it's flipping coins or international relations, negotiation works best when all sides win and want to continue the relationship in the future. Lee Iacocca has recently seen the value of building and maintaining relationships with Chrysler's suppliers as a significant cost-cutting mechanism. Iacocca says that Chrysler must cut its yearly costs by at least $1 billion in order to stay competitive. The largest savings, he says, will come from asking parts and equipment suppliers to join with Chrysler in cost-cutting. His statement indicated that he needed help, not that he was making a demand. He said that both Chrysler and the suppliers would sit down at the negotiating table and figure out how to create a partnership where cost-cutting would increase profits for both sides. A joint program of cost reduction and value analysis is far more effective than an adversarial relationship in which a company asks a supplier for a one-time only price decrease as Chrysler did the previous year. A win/win partnership, in fact, is both a long- and short-term objective.

Gary Karrass, in *Negotiate to Close*, uses a story about two sisters who both want the last orange in the fruit bowl to illustrate this win/win principle. It seems that a parent comes along in this story and divides the orange in half. The wisdom of Solomon, you might say. It turns out however that both sisters are unhappy. One sister wanted only the peel in order to bake a pie. The other wanted the pulpy fruit itself to eat. Neither side won.

Herb Cohen, in *You Can Negotiate Anything*, tells a similar story about his two sons fighting at dinner over the last baked potato. Herb wisely cuts the potato in half. It turns out that one son wanted only the potato skin to eat while the other son wanted only the insides. Neither side won.

I have my own story. My two sons always fought over the last few Oreos in the bag. I'd do what Cohen or Karrass would do. Give two cookies to one son and two cookies to the other one. What a great negotiator I was! Wrong. They would still fight. Mark only wanted the white cream filling, while Kevin wanted only the chocolate cookie itself. It wasn't until we sat down one day and figured out a way for Kevin to get the cookie and Mark to get the filling that peace finally reigned. Peace came when both sides won, that is, when both sides had their wants and needs met.

Here's another example of win/win negotiations. I was working for a company where we were trying to second source a product in Japan. Our primary source found out what we were doing and was greatly upset that we were going to take part of the volume of ordered material away from them. We tried to convince them that even though a second source was taking a part of their volume, they would be able to work on the next generation of the product. Eventually, we solved the problem together by suggesting that the primary source license (for a fee) a second source. To cement this win/win partnership, we also guaranteed that the majority of volume would always go to the primary source. In the event of severe schedule changes, we would begin ordering from the second source per our supplier agreement. Win/win agreements can be fashioned in all types of negotiations.

WHAT THIS BOOK IS ABOUT

I know there are a lot of books out there on the subject of negotiation. So far, I've mentioned the two which were written by Herb Cohen and Gary Karrass. Before you finish reading, you will have heard about several more books. All of the books mentioned in these pages are excellent sources of information. I have used them repeatedly myself. But, as I read them, I began to realize that they were focused on the individual. They advised the individual buyer or seller on how to get a *better deal*. None of them discussed how an entire company can orientate itself in order to get the best possible deal. There was, in short, no book on devising, implementing and maintaining *a company-wide strategic plan for negotiation*. There was no book which told company executives and their managers and employees how to integrate new and proven methods of inventory management, quality control, supplier base management, process control, set-up reduction and so on. Each and every one of these innovations in management philosophy is a powerful cost reduction tool. A supplier, who uses these innovations and who can guarantee 100% on-time delivery, 100% quality and 100% accurate quantities, has a lot of negotiating clout because the emphasis is being placed on cost, not price.

This book provides a new concept to fill the void in the current literature available about negotiating in a World Class and global marketplace. I've hinted that the first area we will cover is the development of a company strategy based on Total Cost, not pricing; Total Quality Control, not inspection; Just-In-Time Delivery; Supplier Certification, or conformance to requirement; and Statistical Process Control, or the "how-to" method. Other areas which will be covered are as follows:

- Structuring procurement to support World Class requirements.

- Developing a partnership with suppliers and customers based on proven cooperation and trust.

- Stating requirements for strategic planning and negotiation.

- Using negotiation tactics in a win/win environment.

THE STRATEGY

The best overall business strategy is one which ends with the achievement of a partnership and World Class Status, as discussed in my book, **WORLD CLASS:** *Measuring Its Achievement* (PT Publications, Inc., Palm Beach Gardens, FL). This is a level at which win/win partnerships are established with both suppliers and customers. Such a strategy would place your company in the best position for planning and executing a negotiating strategy.

This is what we believe a company should want from suppliers in order to become partners in the establishment of World Class companies:

NOTICE

**When your company wants
to sell products to our company,
be sure that your strategic plan
complements our business requirements
and that we will want to establish
a long-term partnership with you.**

The Wisdom of the Nineties	**The Wisdom of the Past** (no longer relevant today)
1. The type of business you pick doesn't matter. Winners can be found in car washes, grocery stores and textiles as well as hardware, pharmaceuticals and information technology.	1. The way to outpace the competition is to discover the fastest growing industries.

The Wisdom of the Nineties	The Wisdom of the Past
2. The objective of the "small is beautiful" philosophy is to create and nurture riches.	2. Size is extremely important for growth. Locate and infiltrate the largest markets.
3. Create new products and processes through innovation.	3. Attain economies of scale by utilizing the experience curve.
4. Value and quality are the foundation of winners with no losers.	4. Lower prices translate into higher market penetration.
5. Expand your business into related products and markets.	5. Discover new business by diversifying.
6. Develop Employee Involvement Programs.	6. Your employees are waiting for you to tell them what to do.
7. The mission of your company should be long-term growth.	7. Short-term results should be a company's primary mission.

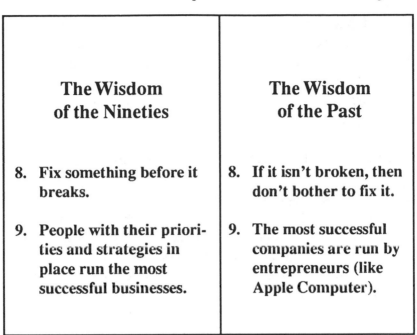

The Wisdom of the Nineties	The Wisdom of the Past
8. Fix something before it breaks.	8. If it isn't broken, then don't bother to fix it.
9. People with their priorities and strategies in place run the most successful businesses.	9. The most successful companies are run by entrepreneurs (like Apple Computer).

Planning for negotiation is a strategy not normally followed. Let us provide you with an example of strategic negotiation planning which involves my executive assistant, Leslie. One morning, she walks into my office and says that she is interested in buying a condominium. After a little discussion, we determine how much money she can afford to spend. I suggest that her first assignment is to go to a bank and prequalify for a loan in order to determine her borrowing power. This will greatly help her in getting the seller to reduce the purchase price by being able to close quickly on a unit.

The next step in her negotiation strategy was to find all the properties in her price range and determine the opening bid and each incremental bid before looking at the property. I pointed out to her at this point that she should not become attached to a piece of property since it was her first purchase and she would probably be selling it in a relatively short time in order to buy a better piece of property. My advice was to treat the purchase as a short-term investment and that she should be willing to walk away if her planning strategy objectives were not met.

After a week of looking at condominiums, Leslie settles on two units, a first and second choice. The next step in her strategy is to get information about the sellers. It turned out that her second choice proved to be the condominium to pursue. The owners had purchased a new home and were facing the prospect of paying two mortgages in 60 days. Furthermore, compared to prices paid on units in the last six months, we determine that the unit is over-priced and being sold in a down market.

As for the actual bargaining, we stuck to the win/win approach — we conceded that the seller will not accept a bid they can't live with and Leslie wouldn't buy unless the price was within her budget. Her offer was both fair and firm and based on the work she had done in her strategy planning. It turned out that she ended up paying slightly less ($500) than what she planned. In retrospect, this was her strategy:

Plan the Strategy	**Method and objectives**
Conduct Research	**Know what you can do**
	It's like having money in hand
Be Patient	**Don't be afraid of "no deal"**
Be Fair	**Be reasonable, but firm**

How many buyers spend the time to develop a strategy like the one on the preceeding page? The best time to negotiate is when you have the time and are prepared. The worst time is when you have a requisition with no lead-time and you must buy now.

THE CHANGING ROLE OF PROCUREMENT

Perhaps the most compelling reason for developing a strategic negotiating plan for your company is that the world of purchasing is changing so rapidly. The emphasis on win/win partnerships and the impending demise of the Three Bid system, Purchase Price Variance (PPV) and Economic Order Quantity (EOQ) is forcing purchasers to seek new methods and techniques. Another important development is that buyers must be conscious of all disciplines within a company and within the companies of their suppliers and customers. What we have seen recently is a large number of requests from clients to develop a Total Cost model to replace PPV. Other companies, such as Rockwell International, have developed supplier rating systems which tie into a Total Cost model.

The negotiation process places a greater demand on a purchaser's professionalism and understanding of the customer's requirements, engineering, quality, manufacturing, finance and the supply base. No longer does a buyer simply place an order or give it to the lowest bidder. The purchaser must be part of a team which plans a strategy and program for ensuring the acquisition of quality items, delivered on-time at the lowest total cost. To achieve this, the buyer must become an expert negotiator.

Worldwide innovations and developments in management philosophies are presenting companies with opportunities for creating long-term relationships with suppliers and customers. Companies which hope to survive and prosper in the future must start with a strategic negotiating plan based on the principles of a win/win partnership. When a supplier increases profits and you decrease costs, that is win/win. That is when there are rewards for both sides and when a motivated supplier becomes a partner. Thus, a negotiator's role now is to attain long-term agreements with value analysis techniques included for cost reduction.

For instance, we recently participated with a client in awarding a five-year purchase order to a supplier in which we used these techniques. The condition of this agreement was that both parties agreed to a value analysis approach in which there were six months allotted to increase the supplier's profit and decrease our costs. All of the crucial negotiations on this contract occurred upfront. This is the essence of win/win negotiations.

HOW TO GET THE BENEFITS OF PARTNERSHIP

The goal of negotiating in most situations is to develop a long-term, profitable relationship with your suppliers and customers.

This is accomplished most easily when there is a strong, clear commitment on both sides to see that *all* needs are met. One way to judge the strength of commitment is to measure the results of each supplier's efforts. Each supplier must continuously demonstrate results and their commitment to satisfy customers. In other words, suppliers (and remember that you are a supplier to your customers!) must conform to customer requirements. A supplier must have a visible track record of participation in cost reduction, on-time delivery, total quality control, accurate counts, and 100 percent quality all the time.

John and Bill Essman of Essman Screw Products, Bryan, Ohio, recently attended a Supplier Certification seminar which Peter Grieco was conducting for the Society of Manufacturing Engineers (SME). The Essman's were at the seminar with the chief purchasing agent of one of their principal customers. At one point in the seminar, we were discussing partnerships and long-term commitments. John told me that his company, which has a small sales volume, recently received a ten-year blanket purchase order for over three times its annual sales volume. The ten-year commitment was certainly a vote of confidence made by both parties. Our best to both of them.

We suggest to our clients that as customers they should demand a defined cost reduction program in order to manage product total cost. They now track supplier performance in the following categories — delivery, capacity, product reliability, cost, quality, cooperation, etc. The goal, which cannot be accomplished overnight, is to move toward the delivery of material which conforms to customer requirements — *no returns or rejects*.

We believe that a partnership exists when there is a commitment to share savings 50/50 with a supplier for value analysis ideas which they suggest. Traditionally, partnership has been defined as a long-term relationship, quality, price and delivery. The chart below demonstrates what we mean:

Present Cost — Old	New Formula— Share Savings with Supplier
Supplier Cost Profit $ 1.00 10% .10	$1.00 Old Cost - .60 New Cost $0.40 Savings
Cost Reduction — Old Supplier Cost Profit $ .60 10% .06	Cost Reduction — New Split Savings 50/50

In this example, a supplier is encouraged to pursue cost reduction techniques and suggestions. The example above results in a savings of 40 cents for both you and the supplier. How many professionals are trained to work in this type of environment? This arrangement is far better than the old 2x4 method: "Hit them until they agree!" A true partnership will split the savings of 40 cents in half. The net result is a supplier who makes a greater profit and a customer who procures an item for a lower cost.

NEGOTIATING FOR QUALITY

The importance of quality can never be underestimated. A production line stopped by a defective eighty-nine-cent ($0.89) part is costly. Companies in the past have tried a number of ways to ensure quality from their suppliers. Most have used a quantifiable measurement such as AQL (Acceptable Quality Level, or jokingly called *A Quick Look*). An AQL approach is no longer acceptable in either a Just-In-Time or traditional environment where quality is the focus. Your negotiating goal today is to accept nothing less than components and assemblies which comply to your requirements.

AQL requirements are expensive. Let's say that you are a buyer for a hotel planning to open a new wing. You order 50,000 square feet of carpeting for the entire new area. With an AQL of 2 percent, you will end up with either 49,000 square feet of usable carpeting or be forced to order 51,000 square feet Just-In-Case. Now you may be ready to open your new wing. We need to look toward quality improvement programs for suppliers. One such program which should be high on your negotiating "want list" is Supplier Certification.

NEGOTIATING FOR SUPPLIER CERTIFICATION

In order to assure improvement in a company's total quality control process, procurement must negotiate for Supplier Certification. This means that you must help your suppliers improve their quality process. Philip B. Crosby probably confused many of us when he wrote *Quality is Free* (McGraw-Hill, New York). If it's free, then the implication is that we don't have to address quality and that buyers should just negotiate on price.

The question I ask is whether your company would pay 10% more for a product that meets your requirements 100% of the time with 100% on-time delivery directly to work-in-process. The lack of emphasis on discussing quality with suppliers and taking action reminds me of the time when Steve Jobs told all of our suppliers at the Apple Macintosh Supplier Symposium to sign up on a poster if they were committed to ship quality products to Apple. Of course, no supplier refused to put their name on the list. But the promise alone was not enough.

The negotiation process ***must*** achieve a sound method for gaining a supplier's commitment to quality. Not words, but action. This action must be a team effort led by Purchasing.

Procurement must be able to purchase components, materials, maintenance and repair, or any other item with the assurance that quality and conformance are part of the agreement or contract. This subject is discussed in **JIT PURCHASING:** *In Pursuit of Excellence* (PT Publications, Inc., Palm Beach Gardens, FL).

Another goal of Supplier Certification is to adjust from the philosophy of stock items to the philosophy of ship-to-WIP (work-in-process). Supplier Certification will only work when you make a total company commitment to quality and back-up that statement with action. In a Supplier Certification environment, there will be little or no excess inventory sitting around. Ideally, we must work toward delivering a quality product or component directly to the line, rather than to a receiving or inspection area. This will mean making delivery schedules part of the negotiations. They will lead to a procurement agreement in which the supplier guarantees delivery performance to your specifications. A buyer's awareness of a company's material requirements and production schedules will guarantee flexible or stable schedules in the future as corporations move toward the buyer/planner concept. It is well to note that many companies are already moving in this direction which depends upon partnership and sound supplier relations supported by buyer/planners.

Negotiation for quality requires the consistent delivery of defect-free parts. The only chance to achieve higher levels of efficiency and productivity will be to make a major change in supply base management. Supplier Certification will also lead to the frequent delivery of smaller quantities of material which will reduce lot sizes, lower inventory levels and reduce work-in-process levels.

These effects on the internal activities of our companies will not work without dramatically better relations with our suppliers. If our suppliers do not know how to reduce set-up time, we must be willing to teach them. Without a reduction in set-up time, small lot sizes are not economically feasible. Agreements with suppliers should state that set-up time will be reduced by 75 percent within a period of time to which both sides agree. In order for them to meet our frequent delivery schedule and our demand for zero-defect parts, we must be willing to make long-term commitments, share engineering technology, get involved early, share profits and develop a partnership with each supplier. Supplier quality is a continuous improvement process in which each supplier is developed in order to contribute to the design quality improvement process.

SUPPLIER SELECTION

SUPPLIER CERTIFICATION: *Achieving Excellence* (PT Publications Inc., Palm Beach Gardens, FL), co-authored with colleagues Michael W. Gozzo and Jerry W. Claunch, is a complete guide to setting up your own program. The process begins with identifying suppliers best able to participate in the program.

Supplier selection which establishes a partnership for negotiation starts with workable definitions of quality for every major product you purchase, including parts, components and materials. You will need considerable input here from your Quality Assurance staff. Use a form like the one shown in Figure 1-1. As you can readily see, these specifications and standards will become an important part of the total package you negotiate.

Now take this list and discuss its contents with the production group or team. Is everything you have listed necessary? Could

**RECORD OF MOST SIGNIFICANT
QUALITY CHARACTERISTICS**

Description of purchased material or part _____

QUALITY CHARACTERISTIC	APPLICABLE SPECIFICATIONS AND ACCEPTANCE STANDARDS (Spec. or Print Number)

Name _____ Date __/__/__

FIGURE 1-1

some of these quality characteristics be deleted without having an impact on production or the final product? The point we are trying to make here is a very important one in negotiation. You should not be wasting time and negotiating power fighting for or over characteristics which are not important to your company.

Next, you will need to know the current quality of the product being received. You can obtain this information from Receiving Inspection or from Quality Deficiency Reports such as the one shown in Figure 1-2 which can be used as an example when developing a similar report for products from your company's suppliers. The Quality Deficiency Report shows the nature of quality problems, who reported them and what, if anything, was done to correct them. A word of warning: If you have selected a product with a perfect track record, make sure you determine whether the product continually met specifications or the report data is inaccurate.

At this point, you have two itemized lists for a selected part or material. Number one — a list of the most significant quality characteristics. Number two — a list of quality deficiencies which have actually occurred. Now, compare the two lists. It is highly likely that you will find some reported deficiencies for characteristics on the first list. What does this do for your negotiation? It provides you with information to ask questions which you can back up with evidence. For example: Why can the supplier meet some quality characteristics but not all? What does a supplier need to do in order to meet other quality requirements? In short, your list of what you want is narrowed down to those areas in which quality is not now being met.

Let's jump ahead for a moment and assume you have reached an agreement. Now you need to monitor a supplier's performance. A Supplier Quality History Record such as the sample shown in Figure 1-3 is useful for compiling this data. You might consider putting this information into your computer system, especially if your company uses the raw data to generate other types of reports. Such reports, when combined with the Quality History Record,

REPORT OF QUALITY DEFICIENCIES				

PURCHASED PART   _____

SUPPLIER   _____

END ITEM   _____

TIME PERIOD COVERED   _____

DATE	REPORTING UNIT	QUANTITIES	DESCRIPTION	DISPOSITION (note seriousness)

Prepared by _____ Date __/__/__

FIGURE 1-2

are powerful negotiating tools. They represent incontestable facts.

Here's a method we recommend to track supplier corrective actions for defective products or rejects. I kept a file folder at my

SUPPLIER QUALITY HISTORY RECORD

SUPPLIER NAME _____ PLANT LOCATION _____

Date Rec'd	Purchase Order No.	Material/ Part No.	Quan. Rec'd	Quan. Acc'd	%	Reason for Rejection	Disposition and Action

FIGURE 1-3

desk for each supplier. When I met with a supplier prior to the next negotiation period, I would pull out the file and say, "Let's discuss what you have done to correct the issues identified in the last report?" Use your power in negotiating to get better quality. A dollar saved through better quality goes directly to the bottom line of your company.

WHO SHOULD YOU SELECT TO WORK WITH FIRST?

Frequently, clients ask me "Which suppliers should we work with first?" I always tell the story of Tom Melohn at North American Tool and Die Company who was recently highlighted in Tom Peter's book, ***Thriving on Chaos***. When Tom Melohn started his company, he targeted 25 companies he wanted to do business with. One of these companies was Digital Equipment Corporation (DEC) where I was working at the time as the Materials Director. Melohn calls up Digital one day and states, "I'm not looking for any orders. I would like a half-hour of your time so you can define what you want from a supplier."

We make an appointment to list what DEC wants from a supplier. A month later, we receive a follow-up call.

"I recently completed a business plan. Will you take an hour to critique it?"

I tell him I would be glad to look it over and make some comments for him. A month later, he calls again.

"I wrote a final draft of my business plan. Will you take a look at it?"

By now, I can't refuse. I'm interested in what he's doing. I look at it, make some comments and send it back. Two weeks later, it's Tom Melohn on the phone again.

"Can I have an order to see if my plans work?"

I can't say "no." I'm hooked. We've worked together for the past two-and-a-half months and developed a relationship. That's the type of supplier you want to work with first: one who is committed and concerned with doing it right the first time. (Quality at the Source.)

My suggestion since then has always been to start negotiating long-term, win/win agreements with the suppliers with whom you have the best relationship, the best quality, the best cost. Work closely with these suppliers first. Help them reduce costs and improve quality and delivery to zero-defect levels. You have a far better chance of winning with the best and a far better chance of gaining substantial savings early in the program. The experience you gain by working with the best will help you work with the more difficult suppliers.

A STRATEGIC PLAN FOR NEGOTIATING

The importance of the purchasing function and the need for negotiating skills was made abundantly clear to me when I worked at Apple's Macintosh plant. We ran a highly successful World Class program there. We built a maximum of 2,000 computers a day (one every 27 seconds) and had no raw material inventory or finished goods warehouse and in excess of 25 turns of inventory a year. Product was built to customer demand and the pipeline was adjusted accordingly. The program's success was directly attributable to the satisfactory negotiation of quality, quantity, delivery and cost in combination with our suppliers.

The trend is for a significant expansion of the negotiating function into areas beyond simply price. Negotiating will play a vital role in balancing the diverse elements needed to make a profit in a time of rapidly changing technology. No longer does a purchaser merely place orders. He or she negotiates with suppliers for engineering, manufacturing and financial capabilities, for internal process control, for design and technical expertise, for JIT delivery and for many more characteristics which were not considered in the past when high levels of inventory covered up all our mistakes. Purchasing is now a process of negotiating with suppliers and developing internally a strategic plan to build products to customer satisfaction. Negotiating, then, is something we must always keep in mind as we design, purchase, build and sell. Negotiating is a strategic tool which will keep us on target for the overall strategic plan of the company.

CHAPTER TWO

"Negotiation is a process, not an event."

— Peter L. Grieco, Jr.

EFFECTIVE NEGOTIATION TECHNIQUES

The good negotiator must be aware of each of the five stages of the negotiating process because each stage requires different strategies and approaches. The five stages of negotiating are:

STAGES OF NEGOTIATION

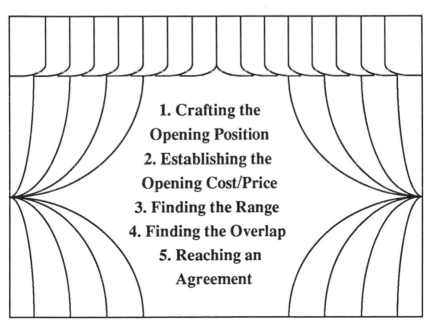

1. Crafting the Opening Position

2. Establishing the Opening Cost/Price

3. Finding the Range

4. Finding the Overlap

5. Reaching an Agreement

STAGE 1: CRAFTING THE OPENING POSITION

The basic tenet of negotiating is to give nothing away unless you are completely aware of the implications of doing so and only if you have balanced those implications against the reasons for giving away the item being negotiated. We all have a tendency to give away more than is necessary because we don't want to be perceived in a negative way. But, throughout a negotiation, you must be on your toes and keenly aware of your *self-interest* and the purpose of the negotiations.

If you give something away, you should be aware of its value. That's because you want something of equal value in return. Unless you communicate what you're giving to the other person at the negotiating table, he or she may not be aware of its value to you. If you allow them to remain ignorant of that information, your goodwill gesture is for nothing. In the eyes of the other person, you haven't given anything away. Let them know that you have. Every time you give something up, you want to be certain that the other person understands that you have done so and that you have given away something of value.

When you communicate value to a supplier or another party, you must identify the value. Value might be terms of payment, letters of credit, cash, trade, or another item. It can even be the right to use your company's name in their marketing literature if they become a supplier of certified parts to your company. Clearly, the other party must recognize the value and agree that it is transferring.

Negotiating Style

Whatever negotiating style you have or choose, you must be

objective and in control. For example, you may want to assume the posture of a "pushover." By appearing "easy," you may win a more favorable contract than otherwise. Our point is that you should go ahead with this style as long as you are aware of what you are doing and in control of what you are doing. And you should know that it's a posture. Just like an actor, you assume a role, or posture, to convey an attitude. But, like an actor, don't be pushed or pulled out of your role by any kind of heckling or tactics from the other side of the negotiating table. Don't make emotional responses! Stay cool. Count to ten. Keep thinking about what you are doing.

In addition, don't feel locked into a role and give it a chance to work. You want to get to the point where you can move from one role to another without the change being noticeable. That reminds us of the time Nikita Khrushchev was addressing the United Nations some time ago. He started his speech by playing the role of the USSR being a helpless country that nobody had to fear. Not too many minutes later, however, he was pounding the podium with his shoe to drive home a point he was making. He had changed roles in order to make a negotiating point. What we still wonder is where that shoe came from. He reportedly still had both of his shoes on when the speech was finished. (What a prop!)

Another key point to address in your negotiating style is building an appropriate relationship with the other side. If you're someone who is urbane, then be urbane. If you're with someone who likes a good, hard, tough negotiation, then be hard, tough and fair. If you're with someone who likes a more personal relationship, then develop a personal relationship.

This reminds us of a story we heard about the writer Tom Wolfe (author of *Bonfire of the Vanities*). At one point in his career, he had to interview the Hell's Angels, so he dressed up appropriately. They didn't trust him. Here was this very cultured fellow in black leather and jeans and they weren't going to say a word to him. Wolfe saw what was wrong. He came back in his traditional white linen suit and acted like the Virginia gentleman that he is. Now the Hell's Angels trusted him and would talk. They saw that Wolfe was being his real self.

It is very important that you play the role with which you are comfortable. At Professionals for Technology Associates, Inc. (PRO-TECH), for instance, I have never forced consultants to sell if they felt that they couldn't. I told them to share leads with other consultants or an officer of the company. One of these people would pursue the lead. And then I guaranteed them that they would get a reward for any lead which resulted in closure.

If you are not comfortable in the role you must play while doing business with a particular company, then seriously consider whether or not you should be the negotiator. The same question applies to any other person who is called upon to negotiate with suppliers or customers. Frequently, you or a team member may not interface well with a supplier. When this happens, substitute another person from your team whose style best matches the style and expectations of the party on the other side of the negotiating table.

Once an appropriate match has been made, there are several techniques to use which will make negotiation more effective. Make casual conversation in order to establish an environment for success. Your purpose should be to increase the trust factor early in the negotiation process. When a person jumps right into the thick of negotiations, this only raises the natural defenses of the other person. In a win/win negotiation, you should show your respect for the other person while establishing your own credentials. Don't forget to listen. The more we learn about the other person's requirements, the better equipped we are to satisfy their needs. Perhaps even more important, the better we know a person's needs, the less apt we are to offer more than is required or to offer them something which they will not consider valuable.

Another technique to use while negotiating is to avoid looking aggressive. You should let the supplier or customer know — through dress, action and words — that you are firm. Don't bend over backwards.

When you are in a negotiation with salespeople who fight over every detail, you may also decide to fight over every detail. If you don't, they may think you are weak — a pushover — and you may wind up with a less than desirable contract. Be like Felix the Cat when you are negotiating. Felix would reach into his bag of tricks and pull out the one trick appropriate to the circumstances. While "tricks" does not sound proper, adapting to the situation is a flexible negotiating style and a strategically powerful tool.

In fact, the ability to vary your style is extremely important in the negotiation process. For your opponents to adjust their style in order to combat your style is the most difficult obstacle they will face. It is the hardest attribute of a person to adjust. If people know your strategy, they will build the cost into the process of negotiation at the very start. If you cannot adjust your style, it may turn the negotiations into a battle which will be costly to both sides.

To use a strategy of asking for an extra one-half percent effectively, you may have to carry out the bluff to go elsewhere. Sometimes, you will have to get up from the table and walk away. When caught bluffing (and if you use this ploy, you will get caught), then make a joke on yourself about it. Self-effacing humor can often gracefully extricate you out of an otherwise embarrassing situation. Negotiation is definitely a poker game. The important thing is not only what you have in your hand, but what the other person thinks you have in your hand! You must distinguish between what you are bringing to the negotiations and what the other side perceives.

STAGE 2: ESTABLISHING THE OPENING COST/PRICE

Although we will talk about cost and price in this stage, keep in mind that often it is not the most important item to negotiate. For our purposes, however, we will use cost and price in this discussion since they are more readily quantifiable than other negotiating objectives. Other objectives such as quantity, level of quality, engineering design support and delivery time will be of major importance in the future.

Your company's opening offer provides the other side with an understanding of your position. In other words, don't price yourself out of the ballpark or price yourself so low that you lose money. If $15 is the highest price you are prepared to offer, then you must decide at what amount to start. If you start at $10, does that mean you are likely to end up at $12? On the other hand, if you offer $6, you might be perceived as an unreasonable person with whom it is best not to do business. You should start with a cost which permits response and is realistic enough to leave room for negotiation. You can always go up in cost, but it is difficult to go down. What you have to do is fall within an upper and lower limit, or planning range, in order to be successful.

When Paul was a Materials Manager for a manufacturer of stereo cartridges, he was looking for a supplier to produce a component. As part of his strategy, he decided not to tell them what price he wanted. Instead, he informed them that they should know what price to quote since they knew the market better than he did. Paul was currently paying $0.26 each FOB Switzerland, freight collect. His goal was to get $0.24 each FOB delivered, freight collect. Unknown to the new supplier that Paul contacted, the Swiss supplier was in the process of buying one of the competitors of the company for which Paul worked. His CEO did not want to give business to a competitor. Paul was told to find a new source at any cost. His gut feel for the situation with the new source was to let them make the first move. Since he knew that they wanted the business, his approach was for them to take one good shot at winning the business. The result was a quote by the new source for $0.22 each, FOB delivered, freight prepaid and allowed for 40,000 units per week. Their quote came in below the range that Paul felt could be achieved. His gut feeling was to keep his mouth shut and the strategy paid off.

STAGE 3: FINDING THE RANGE

If you start off with an opening bid or position that is already your highest acceptable price, there is no room for negotiation. Without a range, you have a non-negotiable offer in which a supplier, for example, informs you that "this is the price and if you want the item, pay what we are asking." (As you shall see in a later section, however, there is really no such thing as a no-negotiation situation.) Either you or your supplier may think that your non-negotiable offer is a fair price, but remember that a fair price is what the market is willing to bear for goods or services rendered.

Fair price has a range. If you are the seller, a price that is below your costs is not a fair price. A price that is above what the other person is willing to pay for value delivered is not a fair price. Between these two extremes exists a range. The point of negotiation is to establish a range which is fair to both sides and which satisfies both parties.

There are negotiations in which the range is very narrow. That happens when the minimum that the supplier is willing to accept and the maximum you are willing to pay barely overlap.

Use caution when finding the range of acceptability so that you don't work against yourself when you set your opening position. You want the supplier to come back with an offer. If you set your opening too high, you have given away negotiating space without getting anything in return.

An example of a narrow range is the situation which occurs when a retail store chain purchased lawnmowers. The margin of cost between the finished product and the consumer price is not very much over the OEM's (Original Equipment Manufacturer) cost. In order to make any money in this business, a retail store must sell a significant volume of lawnmowers because of the low profit margin. Its intent is to sell a low margin item. It does this knowing that shoppers will buy other items of small value, but higher margin during the same visit. Most importantly, they hope to gain new customers.

A novel approach to negotiation that we recently came across appeared in a car advertisement in the *San Diego Union*.The advertisement had a banner headline which said: "The Biggest No Negotiating Sale Ever." The copy of the advertisement told readers that all cars would be clearly marked with a "NO NEGO-

TIATING" sales price. These cars were priced to sell, freeing the buyer "of the worry of negotiating for the best deal!" We wonder how many people rushed down to the car dealership for this "deal" in which nobody could negotiate.

STAGE 4: FINDING THE OVERLAP

The fourth stage of effective negotiating is finding the overlap between the supplier's cost/price range and yours. You are looking for the point at which both of you will be satisfied. Knowing your supplier's costs and margins of profit in some detail puts you in position of power. A large part of your strength as a negotiator comes from your command of information both prior to and during the bargaining period. If the supplier has less command of the pertinent information, then you have the advantage and vice versa. In fact, you can drive the best bargain when the supplier has a strong desire to sell and little or no information about your expectations. Under these circumstances, you are more likely to settle at the lower level of your price range.

In negotiating, *knowledge is power*. You must have an intimate knowledge of your purchasing requirements. Knowledge of alternate materials, for example, is just as important as knowledge of what you are buying. Review whether it is possible to buy and use alternates? Was the specification arrived at when certain materials were less expensive than they are now? If you don't know the answers to these questions, then start participating in design review meetings. Remember that effective negotiating is a company-wide effort.

Salespeople *love* to deal directly with engineers (or anybody but the purchasing person) because they have been known to give away sensitive information unknowingly. To make sure this doesn't happen to you, each company should have some policies on salespeople/engineering relationships. Only Purchasing should discuss value, leaving engineering discussions for specifications.

At one plant, Paul had a purchasing manager working for him that used to terrorize some of the salespeople who passed by his window on their way to Engineering. If they did not pay a courtesy call to keep Purchasing informed, the purchasing manager would announce the following in a loud, clear voice:

"Keep Purchasing informed on each and every call or you will <u>never</u> get a purchase order."

Salespeople quickly learned to go to Purchasing prior to and after their visit to Engineering to get components specified.

Only you and your company can determine how much negotiation is necessary. In general, the larger the dollar purchases, the more likely you will invest a greater amount of time in negotiations. When the amount is small, it is likely that you will set your targets so as not to have a long negotiation process.

In the book, *Managing Negotiations* (Prentice-Hall, Inc., NJ), the authors identify five steps in searching for the overlap:

1. Argue (Discuss).
2. Signal.
3. Propose.
4. Package.
5. Bargain.

Before you begin with step one, however, the authors also suggest (and we agree) that you must have clear objectives. One way to make certain they are clearly defined is to use the MIL approach. The initials stand for objectives you:

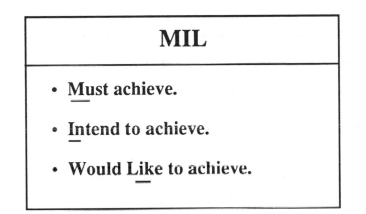

MIL
• **Must achieve.**
• **Intend to achieve.**
• **Would Like to achieve.**

Before entering into any negotiation, we strongly suggest that you write down realistic objectives. Complete Figure 2-1 on the next page for a specific product or commodity you currently purchase. Use the MIL column to make reasonable guesses about what your supplier is looking for. Again, we want to emphasize that a plan must be prepared with a strategy that includes the MIL objectives. Each plan should include what you are willing to give, your fallback positions and your order of counteroffers.

Step One: Argue (Discuss)

The early stages of searching for an overlap typically includes some "feeling out" or actual sparring. At this time, both parties determine what each side is after and has to offer. In this "Argue"

Figure 2-1

Date _____

Product Purchased: _____

Supplier: _____

By: _____ Date: _____

Goals	My MIL			Supplier MIL			What I'm Willing to Give
	M	I	L	M	I	L	
Quantity							
Quality							
Cost							
Delivery							
Terms/Conditions							
Life of Contract							
Payment Terms							
Alternate/Substitute							
Process Improvement							
Cost Reduction Efforts							
Size of Inventory							
Raw							
WIP							
Finished Goods							
Distribution							

step, you and the other party both state what is necessary for a satisfactory agreement and why. You will start to find out if your assumptions about the other side were true and if you have entered negotiations with the correct strategy for a satisfactory settlement. As we shall see in later chapters, there are some "so-called" negotiators who are not willing to bargain. You will have to know how to deal with these people and get them to enter into true negotiation.

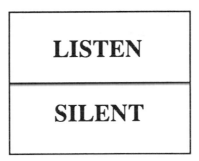

After you state your position, you should **listen** far more than you talk. Listening is where you gain the most information. It is the single most important thing to do during the negotiation process. The Japanese and Russians always have an individual on the their team who is the "designated listener." This person is freed from the responsibility of responding. "Designated listeners" are the ones who call "time out" and fill in the rest of the team on what they missed. The better you have prepared for negotiation, the more you will be able to listen. If you are busy trying to remember information, your mind cannot be actively listening.

If needed, ask questions of the other party in order to get clarification or elaboration of his or her position. This is the point where you begin to look for clues which indicate the other side's commitment to its position. For instance, if your negotiating partner says that your offer is too low and that you are miles apart, then ask what is a reasonable offer. If the response is way above your range, then you ask, "What's the basis for your price? What do you have in mind?" Or, "Why do you think my offer is unreasonable?" The point is to search for more information and to establish an arena of reasonableness.

If the supplier feels that the position is reasonable and you don't, then you have to determine your power level, even if it is a bluff. Herb Cohen, during a seminar, told me that the *perception* of power is an important element in reaching a satisfactory agreement. Some buyers tend to perceive the supplier as having more power than themselves. This is incorrect. The supplier needs to sell to stay in business and you can say "yes" or "no" as easily as he can. You always have the power to take a risk.

You don't have to back down after you have made a reasonable offer which the other person has refused. What do you do then? You say, "That's not reasonable. I don't understand how you arrived at that position. It's beyond my budget. I can't justify that cost. I'm sorry, but we can't deal."

And then be ready to *leave*. If the supplier has been bluffing, you will be asked to "cool down and stay."

One of our clients recently encountered this situation in their negotiations with a large semiconductor house. While meeting at their supplier's plant, a deadlock arose. Our client's team of negotiators packed up and returned to their hotel rooms. Their strategy before they even stepped foot in the supplier's plant was to reach their Design to Cost (DTC) goals. Within ten minutes of their return to the hotel, the telephone rang. Guess who wanted to reopen the negotiation session? The supplier, of course, went back, but with a power shift to our client.

Step Two: Signal

Signaling moves negotiation along by ensuring that a movement towards overlap by one side is matched by a movement from the other side. At some point one of the negotiating parties will need to make concessions. A "signal" is a way to indicate your willingness to concede on a point, if the other side is also willing. You don't want your signal interpreted as surrender.

This is the way a signal works. Let's say that your supplier has just made an unreasonable offer. You have responded that the offer leaves you no room to make a deal and that you, unfortunately, will have to break off negotiations. The person has then asked you to reconsider your position. This is a signal that they may be willing to move away from their extreme position. This tells you that perhaps they came on a little strong, but that they can't afford to make the component or assembly at your price.

"What can you offer?" they ask. "We can't agree to your offer in its present form."

There's another signal. The person has qualified the statement with the phrase, "in its present form."

Now, what do you do once you have received this signal? Don't pull all of your options out of your briefcase and lay them on the table. Send out a signal of your own. Say something like this: "What kind of adjustments can we make in our offer to bring us closer together?" Or, "Are there parts of the offer or the specifications which are particularly costly for you?" Or, "Let's look at some of your major costs. Maybe we can save some dollars there."

Step Three: Propose

Proposing is the stage where you move towards narrowing the gap between the two sides of a negotiation. In negotiating, a proposal is a counteroffer which moves you from your original position, or opening offer. Early proposals should be tentative and concessions should be small. Avoid appearing too eager.

Your proposals should go something like this: "If we trade off the delivery requirements by this much, will you agree to our figure?"

The supplier might say, "No, but I am willing to consider the new delivery schedule to lower the price."

Notice that neither of you have committed yourselves to a specific reduction, but you are agreeing on a way to narrow the gap. You are making a conditioned proposal. You should now be moving from generalities to specifics. Some words of advice here: Be firm on generalities. "You *must* increase your offer substantially!" But be flexible on specifics. "We *suggest* a figure of $30,000."

In *Getting to Yes* (Penguin Books, New York), authors Roger Fisher and William Ury suggest coming up with a BATNA (Best Alternative To a Negotiated Agreement) as a standard against which you test any proposed agreement. As a negotiator, you should have an alternative to the bottom line which usually stops negotiation dead in its tracks. A BATNA stops you from accepting unfavorable terms or from rejecting favorable ones. It answers the question of what to do if you can't reach a negotiated settlement and prevents you from making an agreement at any cost.

If you get a "no" to your proposal, don't reward it with another proposal. Ask for alternatives to your proposal. You may need to coax a response from them at this point. Ask questions like "Do you really need that much time for tooling?" or "Let's talk about some other ways we can review our progress." The point of these questions is to pass the responsibility for the next proposal to the other side. While you are bantering back and forth about different proposals, you are identifying the parts of your proposal that can be adjusted to make both sides happy. By the end of this step, both parties to the negotiations should know what each other wants and what each other is willing to give.

Step Four: Package

Your opening "package" was your most favored position. It sets out your objectives for the ensuing discussion during the arguing step. The ultimate goal is to come up with a package that is win/win to both sides by presenting various proposals. Packaging presents the pieces of your opening offer in a form which more closely matches the other side's interests and limitations. This is the place for some creative thinking. Is there a way to increase the total rewards so that both sides benefit?

An excellent way to resolve issues is through the use of brainstorming techniques in which all the issues are put on the table without any comments. The fishbone on the next page is a good example of this technique. In our book, *Made In America* (PT Publications, Inc., Palm Beach Gardens, FL), we show how to use a fishbone chart to get results in problem-solving sessions. This technique can also be used for negotiation.

This is also the point where the MIL list you prepared before you began negotiations will be utilized. There may be some items on

Design to Cost Goal

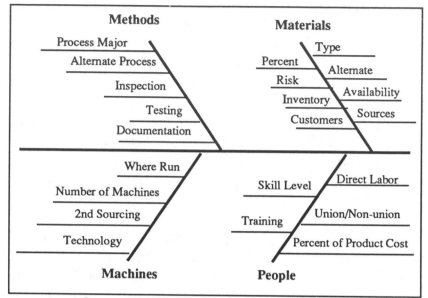

Cause Enumeration Fishbone

this list where you must "hold the line," but there are others where you can bend. Take your "like to get" objectives and use them as concessions in the bargaining session to follow. Before making such a concession, however, ask yourself how much this concession is worth to the supplier and how much will it cost you. Determine and annualize what you want in exchange for each concession before you give it away.

Another way to be creative in packaging an offer is to ask yourself the following questions for each piece of your offer:

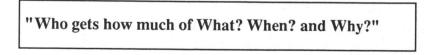

"Who gets how much of What? When? and Why?"

These questions will turn up the variables which can be adjusted to find the overlap. For example, let's say you are discussing Process Improvement. Instead of demanding that the other side substantially improve their quality or accept a lower price, offer to send someone from your Quality Department over to their plant for a period of time in order to help the supplier to fine tune its process control. This alternative, in reality, benefits you as much as it costs you. At the same time, you look like you have made a major concession.

Other techniques for packaging are lengthening the contract, going to a single source, guaranteeing early involvement in future products development, improving payment terms, defining quality requirements for zero-defects or offering terms for the life of the product. Sharing the savings generated by Value Analysis ideas of the supplier will result in significant savings. The more creative ideas you have available for exchange, the better the chances of finding the solution.

Step Five: Bargain

Now you find yourself in the marketplace where, through bargaining, the value of every negotiating element will be established. Everything you give away is in exchange for something you get from the other side. If you feel pressed to agree on a minor concession, be sure to insist upon a minor concession that you are seeking. Bargaining should be a collaborative act. Both sides should be trying to help the other side get what it wants — **without** giving up more than makes you comfortable.

The pivotal word at this point in negotiating is "if." For example: "if you will agree to two deliveries a day at zero-defects, I will agree to pay you each day." When you use "if," the other side is able to discern the value you place on a concession. This type of negotiating is often called *"quid pro quo"* (translated as "this for that") which is a Latin term used when making conditional concessions.

Besides always conditioning an offer with an "if, " never negotiate the elements of your offer as individual items. Keep the pieces of your package linked. Your negotiating objectives are like a bankroll. You want to get agreement on each element before you spend any capital. In this conditional situation, you have not yet agreed to or finalized any contract. You have simply indicated an area where the two parties can reach agreement.

STAGE 5: REACHING AN AGREEMENT

When you sense that a reasonable overlap has occurred, you should push quickly for closure on an agreement on that particular point. This is definitely the time to bring in that creative offer you've been saving: "Look, let's leave the deal as it is. The problem here is minor. We can save that much in inventory carrying costs, if you give me the daily delivery I need."

The strategy at this point is to summarize where both sides stand and to recommend an agreement which represents your final position. Here's another example of a creative closing agreement. You tell the other side that you have already discussed interest rates with your bank.

"They are willing to lend you the money you need for the equipment at only 1/4 percent above prime," you say. "That will more than compensate for the unit price I need. How about it?"

The supplier agrees and everybody comes out a winner. The bank has made a concession to keep your goodwill, you got a unit price below what you were willing to pay and the supplier has financed equipment which will help it get even more business.

It is important when you have reached an agreement to close quickly, formally and legally. Always author the agreement yourself. I hate to write, but I will not let someone do me the favor of writing up our agreement. Once it is in writing, it tends to be the deal and we all interpret things a little differently. Be sure that all parties have the authority to close and sign an agreement.

PARTNERSHIP REQUIREMENTS

Partnership requirements spell out the responsibilities of both the supplier and customer in a win/win relationship. These are the mutually developed requirements you will hammer out together during negotiations. What is missing today is a written statement on what a partnership is all about. Companies talk partnership and practice adversary relationships. We suggest that both you and the supplier draw up a written statement defining partnership.

We need to commit ourselves to working with suppliers to ensure customer satisfaction through total conformance to requirements. At the same time, we should be developing suppliers who are dedicated to the continuous improvement of quality. A partnership requires the ingredients listed in the chart on the next page.

THE CONTENTS OF A SUPPLIER AGREEMENT

This partnership needs to contain certain points which map out

---

KEY PARTNERSHIP REQUIREMENTS

1. Reliability over a period of time, meaning consistent deliveries, product and conformance to customer requirements with proper cost.

2. Quality is the responsibility of the supplier through control of their process, not through inspection techniques.

3. The partnership is based on a long-term commitment with the rules of the relationship defined.

4. Information and data are shared.

---

how the customer and the supplier will integrate their activities. These rules are the operating philosophy for improving the supplier relationship through a win/win partnership which will govern both short-term and long-term activities. The objectives listed in the chart on the opposite page are important.

In order to have a true partnership, each side must be committed to meeting certain responsibilities. This is the core of any successful agreement. Neither side should feel as though they are being taken advantage of. The chart on Page 54 illustrates some of the responsibilities of a partner.

STATISTICAL PROCESS CONTROL

The manufacturing process ideally should be controlled by Statis-

TERMS AND CONDITIONS

- Sets quantity levels for raw material and work-in-process inventories which reflect flexible production schedules.

- Defines quality level as zero-defects.

- Controls price fluctuations and conditions for cost/price changes.

- Establishes delivery schedules and windows as well as shipping terms and packaging specifications.

- Defines terms of payment.

- Establishes responsibilities for corrective action in the event of non-conformance.

- Includes value analysis agreement with joint sharing of savings—the best win/win clause.

- Establishes the frequency and coverage of the forecast.

- Assures the supplier of early involvement in product development.

tical Process Control (SPC) in order to control, check, measure and report the process. We can no longer conduct business in an environment which accepts previous high levels of scrap, rework, waste and delays. We must start to negotiate with suppliers to

NEGOTIATION CRITERIA and RESPONSIBILITIES of a PARTNERSHIP	
CUSTOMER	**SUPPLIER**
1. Process-achievable specifications.	1. Evaluate process capability to meet customer specifications.
2. Clear standards.	2. Evaluate standards/methods.
3. Open line of communication.	3. Feedback mechanism.
4. Notification of organizational changes/policy.	4. Notification of organizational changes/policy.
5. Discussion of potential changes required.	5. Discussion of potential changes in process requirements.
6. Assist supplier in solving quality, production problems.	6. Notify customer of quality, production problems, capacity.
7. Provide timely feedback and corrective action.	7. Provide timely feedback and corrective action.
8. Provide survey results.	8. Notify to survey improvements.
9. Share audit results.	9. Close feedback loop.
10. Resolve supplier questions.	10. Inform customer of new processes and/or materials.
11. Inside contact with response time who can commit to change by name.	11. Inside contact with response time who can commit to change by name.
12. Commit to continuous improvement program.	12. Commit to continuous improvement program.

ensure that SPC will be practiced when required. Negotiating for the supplier to establish process control is the new level of excellence. Statistical Process Control is an effective method of evaluating a process to identify both desirable and undesirable changes. Remember that what is measured is as important as the method or technique used. Although you may already use Acceptable Quality Level (A Quick Look) (AQL), we don't view it as the primary measuring tool for the long run. AQL is an evolutionary step you will go through before you move on to SPC.

CONFORMANCE TO REQUIREMENTS

Much is said about conformance to requirements, but most of it assumes that conformance is exclusively a management problem. We view conformance more broadly. What other questions are implicit in the accepted definition that conformance is a product meeting the requirements set forth by the specifications?

- Does it meet the customer needs?
- Does it meet the Engineering specifications?
- Does it meet the manufacturing process requirements?
- Does the product meet the test requirements?

It pays to make it right the first time, but this requires close communication and documentation of the actions between Engineering and each supplier.

SUMMARY

All the partnership requirements discussed above are what you seek to achieve in the negotiating process. Now that you know the stages of negotiation and what you want in an agreement, let's next review how to prepare for a negotiation process.

CHAPTER THREE

"When you destroy the salesperson, that's Soviet style negotiation. When the salesperson says thanks, that's a powerful negotiation tool."

— Peter L. Grieco, Jr. and Paul G. Hine

PREPARING FOR THE NEGOTIATION PROCESS

Negotiation, as we now know, is a process. It is not a static event, but a lively interchange with all the elements of a mini-drama or play. After all, it has actors, a script and dialogue which leads to a resolution — the mutual establishment of deliverable items at a cost and under conditions which have been agreed upon. Preparing for negotiation is like writing the script for a play. It is often necessary to develop several alternate scripts. If you follow just one script all the time, the negotiator on the other side of the table will find you to be totally predictable.

Some companies are moving toward a very predictable strategy. That strategy is to be open, fair and totally committed to the mutual satisfaction of both parties. They will continue to use this strategy when their partner's behavior is the same.

You are the one who can and should write that script. You are the expert, the professional. You don't want to be a spectator who watches events unfold because when you allow the other side to write the script, you will lose all the advantage and be reduced to a bystander.

WIN/WIN APPROACH

If you know how to structure a negotiation so that it's a win/win for both sides, so that each party gets what they want, the results will be one success after another. Each of these successes comes without the pressure, anxiety and tension that all feel is normal. Negotiation should be fun and an enjoyable experience for all.

The approach for win/win requires establishing a trustful and cooperative attitude in order to achieve continuous success. Negotiation has six paradigms to consider.

SIX PARADIGMS OF NEGOTIATION	
• WIN/WIN	• LOSE/LOSE
• WIN/LOSE	• WIN
• LOSE/WIN	• WIN/WIN or NO DEAL

WIN/WIN — A philosophy and frame of mind that constantly seeks mutual benefit and interaction.

WIN/LOSE — This is an authoritarian approach in which I win, you lose. Negotiators who believe in this approach use credentials, passions or personalities to get their way.

LOSE/WIN — The opposite of win/lose, these negotiators are programmed to lose. Usually, no standards exist for this type of person.

LOSE/LOSE — This situation occurs when two stubborn, thick-headed people get together and let ego or individual interest override common sense in the search for a solution.

WIN — These people don't want someone else to win or lose. They just want to get their way.

WIN/WIN or NO DEAL — This basically means that neither party could find a solution which was beneficial to both. This type can honestly say, "I only want to achieve a win/win solution."

These paradigms center around a philosophy which is based on a total commitment to interaction. We are trying to create a habit of effective leadership that can only negotiate in a win/win style. *Win/win is not a technique.* It is a philosophy which consists of several dimensions considered in an evolutionary flow:

DIMENSIONS OF WIN/WIN

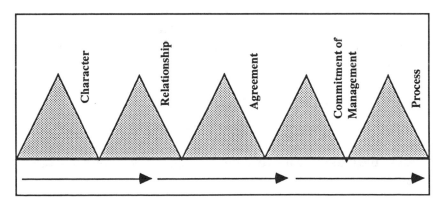

Character — Building a foundation for win/win on high integrity, ethics and trust.

Relationship — Building a relationship around a win/win philosophy. Building on the trust which is required to put our cards on the table.

Agreement — Shifting the negotiation to a strategy where both sides can be partners in success through the use of performance or supplier agreements.

Commitment of Management — Getting the company to adopt a win/win philosophy as a way of life.

Process — Creating an environment where negotiation is a process, not a one-time only event. Building a support network for Continuous Improvement Process.

These five dimensions of win/win create the conditions necessary for instilling the habit of interpersonal leadership within the relations between Purchasing and each supplier. In order for this leadership to get results, both technical and employee involvement are needed. The mutual learning process of two or more partners will result in mutual benefits. Effective win/win negotiation involves a proactive approach with vision, guidance and power.

TRUST AND COOPERATION

Achieving win/win involves trust and cooperation. As the chart shows, the closer we move to the high end of both axes, the closer we are to achieving win/win. Trust and cooperation are the

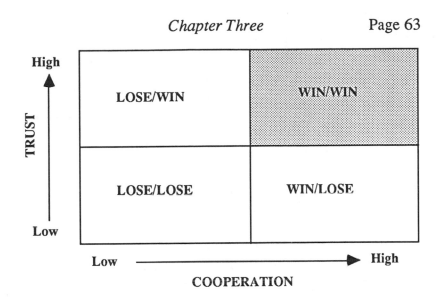

foundation of win/win and everything else builds upon that foundation. Trust requires integrity and maturity.

Stephen R. Corey, author of *The 7 Habits of Highly Effective People* (Simon and Schuster, New York), says that "we have to search within ourselves — beyond scripting, beyond attitudes and behaviors — to achieve validation of win/win."

TYPES OF NEGOTIATION

Negotiation is a technique for the mutual establishment of deliverable items at an agreed upon cost and conditions. This drama unfolds in a micro-marketplace. As in the days of old (and in many places today), the buyer and seller endeavor to reach an agreement which determines the value of specific deliverable goods or services to the buyer. Just like a play, there is a conflict (bargaining) and a resolution (agreement).

In order to prepare for the drama of negotiation, we must determine and define the key elements between the three types of negotiation:

- **Common Practice Negotiation
  — A Ritual of Custom**

- **Real Time Negotiation
  — Partnerships**

- **Non-Negotiation**

COMMON PRACTICE NEGOTIATION — A RITUAL

Picture the scene unfolding in a bustling local farmer's market where a number of merchants are selling and buyers are negotiating for the purchase of oranges. This bargaining can become quite noisy and lengthy even though all the oranges are about the same quality and all the buyers will eventually pay about the same price. In other words, the marketplace may already have fixed a value on a pound of oranges as being $1.50. All the players in this negotiating drama know this fact, but the buyer continues to negotiate. He is participating in a long-established ritual. And he is playing his role to the hilt, because if he doesn't, he may end up paying $1.60 per pound. That's 10 cents more than anyone else because he didn't take part in the ritual.

Ritual negotiation does not happen only in the produce markets of foreign lands. It takes place more often than we notice in the purchases of automobiles and real estate, not to mention in many modern commercial transactions. In the course of doing business as a professional, you must be able to identify the situation and determine whether or not it is useful to enter a ritual negotiation.

On a recent trip to the Bahamas, we had a chance to visit the straw market where people sew, manufacture and sell items to tourists. While there, Susan, the wife of our Vice President, wanted to buy some tee-shirts to take home. Now, you have to understand that Susan is the nicest person in the world and that she is going up against people who bargain every day of their lives. As she went to each of these merchants, they told her that the tee-shirts would cost somewhere between $8 and $10 for each tee-shirt. Finally, she found a woman who wanted only $6 which Sue thought was a great deal.

I happened to pass by at this moment and Sue proceeded to tell me what a great deal she was making. I told her that she should not pay more than $2.50 each. Of course, she said that there was no way she could get them for that price. I explained to her that the lady selling the tee-shirts expected to go through the ritual of negotiation, a norm in her country, but that she knew that most tourists don't understand this ritual. Eventually, we got the price down to $3 each or four for $10.

There are at least two practical advantages you gain from using ritual negotiation. First, by identifying the format and knowing the realities of the situation, you have better control. Second, in the instance where a prospective purchase may be so small, it may not be worth your while to plan a detailed negotiating scenario. If the supplier still wants to negotiate, you should target a ritual negotiation. In this case, you would set your price at 10 or 15 percent lower than you expect to pay. Then, at the supplier's insistence, you reluctantly come back up to the price you wish to pay. Make certain, however, that you get some benefit from the supplier each time you make a concession.

Ritual negotiation does not change the realities of the market-place, but it can offer significant benefits. It can serve certain needs of both parties and can provide great satisfaction if you are aware of the ritual and can control the action behind the scenes.

REAL TIME NEGOTIATION

When the size of the purchase warrants, you will be writing a different negotiating script. A larger stake in the game will necessitate greater care in the preparation of your script. You will need to enter into real time negotiation. The benefits to you will be immediate. You will be able to get what you want at the price you are willing to pay. And, since the supplier has a clear and unambiguous picture of your needs, you will come out ahead in the long run as well.

Having performed the job correctly, you will have made the supplier a partner (instead of an adversary) in the negotiation process. You may even become comfortable enough to allow the supplier to set the stage as they wish. But make sure you write and control the script!

Let's look now at the Japanese style of negotiating. It is an excellent example of the art of real time negotiation. Japanese negotiators are excellent role models. They are patient when they select suppliers to provide them with materials. Most importantly, they take pride in their work and products. They write a negotiating script based on extensive preparation and teamwork. They complete their homework and understand the mechanics and economics of the bargaining process. This creates a powerful bargaining position based on the three key elements of negotiation:

- **Knowledge.**
- **Patience.**
- **Teamwork.**

This should be the basis for your outline as you prepare a negotiating script. With them, you can create a powerful bargaining position.

When the Japanese, for example, negotiate here on our turf, they send over a team of experts armed with knowledge on the products, research on competition and awareness of market shares. They always look at the total product and operate in a patient, professional manner. In contrast, U.S. negotiators tend to focus on the components and seem to be always in a hurry to get results. They do not allow for a patient style of interplay where the necessary time is taken to make the negotiations work.

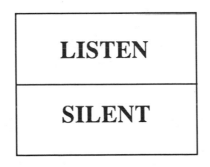

As we noted in the last chapter, the Japanese team also has a designated listener on it. This person does not talk to the customer, so he is free to watch, listen and observe. Much information is gained if we *listen*, and to listen actively, we must be *silent*. As the illustration on the previous page shows, the two words are related since both are spelled with the same letters.

The designated listener will also call timeout in order to fill in information which the team may have missed. These timeouts are often held right in front of the other side as the team switches to speaking Japanese. Effective use is also made of the timeouts. Negotiations are not treated as a 100-yard dash by the Japanese, but more like a triatholon. A triatholon would not be so difficult, of course, if it was spread out over three days. The lesson we learn is not to make negotiation harder than it needs to be. Take breaks when required and pace the process.

EMPHATIC LISTENING

In negotiations, we should first seek to understand which necessitates a shift in paradigm. Usually, we speak to be understood but do not listen with the intent of understanding. A recent conversation with a president of a company about his Purchasing Vice President is a good example of what we are talking about.

President: I can't understand Tom (VP Purchasing). He just won't listen to me at all.

Pete: Let me restate what you said. You don't understand Tom because he won't listen to you.

President: That's correct.

Pete: Let me try again. You don't understand Tom because he won't listen to you.

President: That's what I just said.

Pete: I thought to understand another person, you needed to *listen to them*.

We are often so busy talking that we don't hear the other person. When this president finally got the message, we were able to move on to solve the purchasing issue at hand.

POWER, INFORMATION AND TIME

Power, time and information are the three major elements of the negotiation process. Without these three items working side by side, real negotiation will not happen.

Many of you have heard the CEO of your company at the annual meeting say, "I want my people to kill or destroy our competitors. We want to crush them." This is a very powerful statement which you may, at first, think is not win/win. But it is! It is win/win for your company and suppliers to beat the competition. The CEO's statement implies that "to kill the competition" is to work together as a team to achieve mutual goals. At the Apple Macintosh plant, Steve Jobs was obsessed with "killing" IBM. We were fanatical about being the best computer company in the world. We worked as a team for success. Jobs made us paint IBM robots a different color and remove IBM nameplates. Now, years later, he enters a joint venture with them to market his new machines. And on July 5, 1991, Apple and IBM announce a joint venture in technology and research, heralded by *USA Today* as a win/win proposition.

There are several ways to make power work for you. First, you should recognize and evaluate your opponent, the person with whom you are negotiating in the context of the competition. If there is a lot of competition in the arena, then you immediately have more power. If there is less competition, then your perceived power may be diminished. But there are ways to preserve power even in a sole source situation which we will examine later.

Before starting, establish whether or not the other party has signature authority within their own organization. If they do not, then you may be better off curtailing the negotiation process.

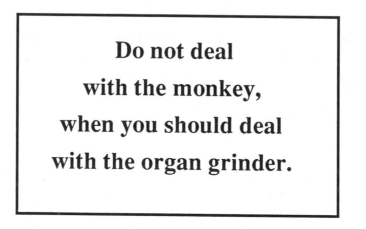

**Do not deal
with the monkey,
when you should deal
with the organ grinder.**

If you try to negotiate in such a situation, it may cost you more than you originally set out to pay since you may be in for a two-tier negotiation. After you have established the authority of your opponent, try to learn about his or her background. Are you dealing with a salesperson or a marketing person? If so be aware that these people have been trained to close. Here's another way to use background to shift power to your area of expertise. If I'm negotiating with an engineering person, I'm not going to banter about engineering matters. (If there are engineering matters which need to be discussed, then it is best handled by an engineer on your team. As a member of the team, the engineer knows the area which should or should not be entered.) I'm going to steer the conversation around to operational matters. That's my forté. If I talk about things you are familiar with, you're going to whip me. The power will shift to your side of the table. That is why you must know about your supplier's manufacturing process. If your opponent says his costs are going up because of your demand for higher quality, do you know enough about quality management to counter? Quality may cost more in the short-term, but in the long-term it will cost 20-40% less. Now what is your price?

It's vitally important to establish your power in the initial session of negotiations by knowing as much as possible about your opponents. You should search out information, especially when dealing with somebody new. "What's your background? How long have you been in your job? ... Oh, you're relatively new. What did you do before this job?" Once you've established this type of background, you have an edge. You can bring about a subtle shift of power. Your opponent may never be aware (and you certainly don't have to let them know), but the power is shifting very, very easily and quietly.

You should also learn as much as possible about the products you want to buy. Include gathering information about the product in our negotiation strategy. Many salespeople know little about the product they are selling. They don't know how it is made or how it works. All they know is that it costs $1.00 and comes in red or blue. If you find out that this is the extent of their knowledge, you might be at a distinct advantage if you have completed your homework in preparing for the negotiations. *Knowledge* will keep power on your side. The other side may be so knowledgeable that they can't negotiate the areas which are most important to you.

Once the negotiations start, we need to establish the legitimacy of an offer presented by the other side. Is it a good offer and does it fit your requirements? Is it reasonable in terms of the initial price? When you have completed your homework, you will know the answers to these questions. You may not have the exact figures, but you'll know something is wrong if the supplier is asking $18,000 for a $12,000 piece of equipment.

Another element of power is risk taking. Before you begin negotiating, you should know how much of a risk you are willing to take. How far will you push a situation before you back down? How far will your opponent push a situation before he backs down? This is similar to gambling in Las Vegas. The more you risk, the bigger the payoff; the less you risk, the smaller the payoff. The point here is that you have to define your risk in order to be properly prepared.

Recently, Pete and Mary were at the tables standing next to a 60-year-old Chinese man. Pete had $200 in front of him and the older gentleman had just cashed a voucher for $2,000. When he received the dice, the man placed $200 on the pass line. Pete put down $10. The man's first roll was a seven, a winner. Before his next roll, he increased his bet to $400 and Pete left his at $10. The man's next roll was a seven as well, another winner. In fact, in less than half an hour, the Chinese man had accumulated over $40,000 in winnings. Pete had won slightly less than $1500 and was starting to wish he had bet just like the man standing next to him.

Upon reflection, however, Pete realized that the risk of his losing $200 was greater than the risk of the Chinese man losing $2,000. In fact, the lucky man eventually passed the dice when he felt his luck changing. He never did crap out.

There are people who would not think of gambling in Las Vegas, yet they are perceived as being big risk takers in the negotiating process. These people know they are not really taking big risks because of the extensive preparation they have done. They know that the risks are minimal. Doing your homework and preparation is the greatest risk reducer at your disposal.

If you enter negotiation cold-turkey without defining your risk, you are going to give ground. So be prepared to say "no deal" if any part of the package does not fit your established criteria.

Setting precedents is yet another way to establish power. Whatever you do in this negotiation sets a pattern for future negotiations. And whatever you have done in past rounds sets a pattern for the current round. Remember that it is very rare to go from a position of power to a negative role and then back to a position of power. If you were previously in the power seat when dealing with a supplier, you will be able to continue in the power seat the next time because a precedent has been set.

> # If you think
> # you have power ...
> # then you have it!

Your attitude also plays a role in your power position. In other words, if you think you have power, then you have it. If you think you don't have power, then you don't. It's simply the power of positive thinking. The perception of having power empowers you.

As Henry Ford said:

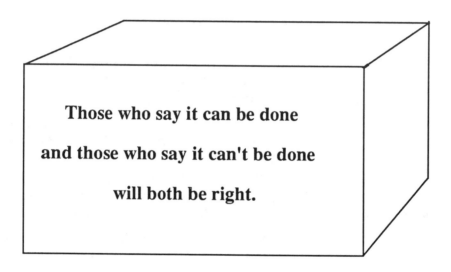

Those who say it can be done

and those who say it can't be done

will both be right.

The Lawler-Porter model of expectancy theory shows that people tend to reach the goals that they believe they can reach.

There is a price we pay for gaining power in negotiations. That price is the substantial investment you make in time, but this investment will pay off in the end. Taking time in the planning stages will bring you dividends. You may have to go to the library to research your product and learn where the material comes from. But you must arm yourself with all the facts. The more time you spend learning about each product, the more you will know. The more you know, the more power you retain.

In order to control power in the negotiation process, you must understand what enables you to influence your opponent. One of your objectives is to find out what the other person wants. What would you do, for example, if a terrorist was holding a hand grenade and threatening to blow up your office? Meanwhile, somebody over the public address system announces that you have to negotiate your way out of this. In this example, it's obvious that the stakes are high, but power works the same way in any negotiating situation. Your first approach is to establish the criteria for communication. Your second step is to search for common ground and to deflect the energy from you to the real problem. Finally, look for a solution which satisfies the other party and, in the case of our example, spares people's lives.

One powerful means to get information is to ask for a tour of your supplier's plant. Most people are very proud and happy to provide such a tour. Indeed, while they love showing off their facilities, you can very quietly pick up a lot of useful information. When I take a tour, I observe things very carefully. I look in corners. I watch for scrap or rework. I watch for rejects. I look for dust. I then store up all this useful information. I go to the receiving dock to find out who their suppliers are and to the shipping dock to find out who their customers are. It will provide power later in the negotiations. If your company formally surveys its suppliers and potential suppliers, it will gain substantial information and be in a good position to help its partners reduce costs.

CHAPTER FOUR

"We must train our people now in order to save dollars tomorrow!"

— Paul G. Hine

PLANNING
FOR
NEGOTIATION

Advance planning and communication are vital to successful negotiation. This becomes clear when we understand negotiation as an ongoing process and not as a static event as many people believe. There is a big difference. Because it is a process, negotiation involves its own lead-time. For example, in planning the negotiation of your purchases, you understandably depend to a great extent on your co-workers. As a purchasing professional, you need to communicate with engineers, users, production line supervisors and material planners, supplier quality engineers (SQE) and others in order to find out what materials are needed, where and when.

COMMUNICATIONS

You must also communicate with your suppliers. You need to keep them informed. You should look to reduce lead-time as much as possible when ordering a product. If a supplier has to work overtime to get an item delivered, you typically pay more. Again, planning is the key. We need to work internally to shorten our planning cycle and externally to shorten our suppliers' lead-times. This will allow each company to serve their customers better.

Furthermore, you also need to factor in quality and scheduling in the planning stage of negotiations. When Steve Jobs, the co-founder of Apple, launched his latest creation, NeXT, his strategy for supplier qualification was quite strict. Using only 50 suppliers (half of the number the usual workstation builder retains) NeXT got its engineers and purchasing people involved in an extensive evaluation of supplier qualification. According to NeXT's Materials Manager, suppliers are major partners whose financial, technical and engineering capabilities are all evaluated. This evaluation process can take from three to five months.

In preparing for negotiations, you will spend time developing a plan as well as getting to know your suppliers. We have to allow this process its own lead-time. Here is a typical scenario:

> You know you're going to come see me in a week. You give me a call and say, "Let's set the parameters for when we sit down. Here's what I would like to talk about. Do you want to add anything to the list?"

> Then you fax me a list of items you want considered and say, "Let me tell you my feelings before we start and what I'm doing on my side. I'd like to see these kinds of things on the table. So, go over the list I faxed to you and when I get there, give me your thoughts."
> What have you done? You've given me an opening

position. You've shared information with me and started the process of negotiation. In a few days, you will probably call me back and ask if I have had time to take a look at the list you faxed to me. I tell you that three of the items are probably okay, but there's a gray area in one. We really don't have a zero-defects program, I explain. But, at least, when we sit down at the negotiation table, I'll be ready because you have shared all this information with me ahead of time.

There are two sides to this information process. One is to gather information and the other is to give it. While I'm feeding information to you, I'm gathering it as well. How much I get back depends upon how much I give you. Here's another example of what I mean:

Currently, I'm dealing with a company where I'm trying to sell an in-house seminar. The president told me what he would like to see in the program. I write the proposal based on his requirements. I write it to include his expressed wants and needs. After I write it and before I mail it, I call him up and say, "Let me read my letter to you." I read it and he says that it is fine, "just what I want." Then I mail out the letter. That is the sharing and giving of information.

This informational give and take actually makes it easier for me to close this deal. There wasn't even a whisper of problem with this client because the seminar was tailored to meet his needs. There never was a chance for an issue to grow. Sharing information takes time, but both sides win if you do. You should expect to gather and provide information before you actually sit down at the negotiating table.

REAL NEGOTIATION

There are two important types of true negotiation with which you should become familiar. The first is cooperative, or win/win, negotiation. The second is competitive, or win/lose, negotiation. Cooperative negotiation is easy. It says that there is always a better

Cooperative	Competitive
WIN/WIN	**WIN/LOSE**

deal if you take the time to build a relationship with your suppliers and customers. Put simply, this process of making the pie big enough for everybody is the new trend in negotiating today. It is commonly referred to as the Expanded Pie Theory of Negotiations as seen on the next page.

Some people can not accept Pie #2, even though their piece is over three times as large. Their mindset will not accept less than 50 percent, no matter how much they stand to gain.

If your negotiation is competitive, you are not building a partnership and that may mean that this round of bargaining is a one-shot

Which would you rather have?

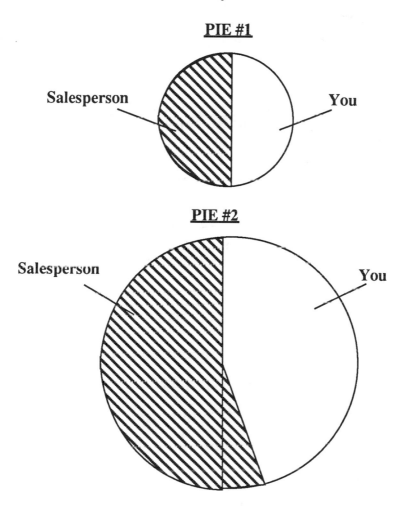

deal. You will antagonize the other side so much that they probably won't want to deal with you again. The key to success in negotiations depends upon your ability to focus on the issues and not the peripherals. Ignore the "smoke" and stick to the issues during negotiation. Make a statement, put your facts on the table and go with them. Don't defend them. Try to make the opposition tell you why they want their needs granted. You become the listener. If you're defending a position, then you aren't listening.

When there's a conflict or a barrier to the negotiation process, don't be afraid to make changes. For example, Tom and I are negotiating and we simply don't get along. We're at an impasse. One solution would be to change the players. Don't be afraid to tell the other side that you want to switch players because there are some personal problems between the two sides. When there is too much conflict, find an alternative way around the problem.

REQUIRED STEPS

Gathering the Facts

Brainstorming

The Team Meeting and Role Descriptions

Mock Negotiation

Planning is a Way to Gain Internal Consensus

The Use of the Written Agenda

TIME AND INFORMATION

There are major advantages to keeping negotiation a process, instead of an event, since we continue to negotiate as things change. We put clauses into contracts if prices go down or volumes go up. Your negotiation plans and store of information should be constantly updated.

Keep a folder on each supplier and what you purchase from them. If you are planning to see a supplier tomorrow, now you know what to talk about — what is the supplier's rating? Quantifiable data on a supplier is invaluable while negotiating. We need to get past feelings and start discussing the performance which the supplier needs to improve.

NEGOTIATING INVENTORY COST

If you are like most purchasing managers, you negotiate and purchase items which are put into inventory. The material requirements schedule generated by Production and Inventory Control or by Material Planning is the basic schedule which initiates the whole process of procurement. But, if their efforts are not coordinated with the Purchasing department, it's a wasted effort. So let's take a look at some of the requirements of inventory.

You, as the purchaser, must ultimately be in control of inventory for your company. If you contract for less than the plant needs, then the production line will grind to a halt. If you contract for a large quantity over a long period of time, you may be insuring that the production line won't halt, but you are overstocking the warehouse with goods which are expensive to store. We think it is important, as a step in the negotiation process, to understand how to calculate the cost of carrying inventory (COI). The COI average for most companies is between 2-3% per month or 24-36% per year. On the following page is a calculation for inventory which has been successfully used.

What we do not want is to pay for either the supplier's inventory

I. STORAGE SPACE COSTS	DOLLARS
1. Taxes on land and buildings for storage	_____
2. Insurance on storage building	_____
3. Depreciation on storage building	_____
4. Depreciation on other warehouse installations	_____
5. Maintenance and repairs on building	_____
6. Utility costs, including heat, light and water	_____
7. Janitor, watchman and maintenance salaries	_____
8. Storage/handling at other locations	_____
Subtotal	_____

II. HANDLING EQUIPMENT COSTS	DOLLARS
9. Depreciation on equipment	_____
10. Fuel for equipment	_____
11. Maintenance and repair of equipment	_____
12. Insurance and taxes on equipment	_____
Subtotal	_____

III. INVENTORY RISK COSTS	DOLLARS
13. Insurance on inventory	_____
14. Obsolescence of inventory	_____
15. Physical deterioration of inventory	_____
16. Pilferage	_____
17. Losses from inventory price declines	_____
18. Storage manpower costs	_____
19. Labor cost	_____
20. Clerical cost	_____
21. Fringe benefits	_____
Subtotal	_____

IV. CAPITAL COSTS	DOLLARS
22. Interest on money invested in inventory	_____
23. Interest on money invested in equipment	_____
24. Interest on money invested in land and buildings	_____
Subtotal	_____
GRAND TOTAL	_____

stocking levels or for ours. Knowing about the cost plays a major role in the negotiating process. We need to remember the new Activity Base Accounting (ABA):

ASSETS	LIABILITIES
PEOPLE	INVENTORY

TASK

The task of management is to lower the cost of operations and products. The buyer can make the job easier by thinking ahead when working up supplier agreements. Unfortunately, the prime selection criteria of many companies today for suppliers is:

- **Price.**
- **Quality.**
- **Quantity.**
- **Delivery.**

Frequently, a purchaser will consider the criteria above in just that order. This is a mistake. The priorities of a purchaser should be in this order:

- **Quality.**
- **Delivery.**
- **Quantity.**
- **Total Cost.**

Quality has to be the number one criterion in selecting and

negotiating with suppliers. Delivery time is becoming extremely important because of the high cost of keeping inventory on warehouse shelves. If a purchaser buys $5 million worth of inventory and holds it for one year, the cost of keeping that material amounts to $1.8 million, or 36 percent of the value of the product. If you held that same material for three years, you would almost be better off throwing it away and taking the write-off. A purchaser should never put him or herself in that position.

Knowing how much inventory you want to carry is extremely important to the buyer. If a "good deal" turns up, the buyer must consider the cost of keeping that item on the warehouse shelf. If the item sits too long, the "great deal" begins to lose value. Knowing how much inventory you have, how it will be used in production and how fast it needs to be replenished are things every purchaser must know in order to plan a negotiation strategy. This is why many companies are switching to the concept of the buyer/ planner or Commodity Line Manager who has "womb to tomb" responsibilities. These people eliminate the middle person and improve communication so that there is finally a focus on respon- sibility, authority and accountability. The professional buyer is not only involved with purchasing, but with inventory manage- ment, the cost of inventory and the cost of quality. The result is a Total Cost approach.

JUST-IN-TIME INVENTORY

Just-In-Time (JIT) inventory radically changes the priorities of purchasing as we have shown in our book, **JUST-IN-TIME PURCHASING:** *In Pursuit of Excellence* (PT Publications, Inc., Palm Beach Gardens, FL). JIT inventory refers to the delivery of raw materials, parts or components just before they are needed in the production or manufacturing process. The exact specifications of JIT vary. Some purchasers negotiate delivery time as delivery on the day it is needed. Others provide themselves a little more leeway. Do not put unnecessary restrictions on your suppliers, unless you can utilize them. The purchaser's goal is for both the customer and supplier to have as little inventory as possible.

Take a close look at the World Class Requirements below. As you can see, you must first have an accurate and responsive planning system. You also need cooperation and coordination between Quality Assurance, Purchasing and the supplier. This is an ongoing relationship with give and take along the way. It requires an open door and an open mind on the part of everyone involved.

REMEMBER:

**A mind is like a parachute.
It only works if it is**

OPEN.

You must also make time for frequent planning meetings and realistic evaluations of supplier capacity planning in line with projected fluctuations.

A number of companies have been less than satisfied with JIT because they have rushed to bring it on line without consulting their suppliers. In effect, these companies pushed their inventory back on to their suppliers. Bring JIT on line slowly. Work closely with suppliers to implement it in a closely monitored phase-in. Have frequent meetings with your suppliers to help them make the transition.

WORLD CLASS NEGOTIATION REQUIREMENTS

1. An accurate and responsive planning system to generate correct requirements to suppliers.

2. Close coordination between Quality Assurance, Purchasing and suppliers as the foundation of a partnership.

3. An open door and an open mind in order for the Continuous Improvement Process to work.

4. Frequent planning meetings. A budget for a minimum of two visits per year to each supplier.

5. Realistic evaluations of supplier capacity planning so that lead-times are short, accurate and can accommodate the required flexibility.

NEGOTIATING TERMS OF DELIVERY

As part of the buying process, each buyer must negotiate terms of delivery. After quality (which was discussed in Chapter 1), delivery is the next most important criteria. The purchaser has a tremendous responsibility to maintain the lowest level or minimal supply based upon frequent and timely delivery of quality components or material. In order to address this level, you must have answers to these questions: What is the geographical location of the supplier? What method of delivery will be utilized?

The trend is toward FOB Delivered, Freight Collect, using a mutually agreed upon carrier. If you want the goods delivered on time, then the supplier should maintain legal responsibility until your company signs for the shipment. That is FOB Delivered. The customer ultimately pays for the freight charge and Freight Collect allows for this charge to be a separate, controllable and negotiable cost. The worst possible scenario is FOB Shipping Point, Freight Prepaid and Billed. In this case, your company legally owns the shipment as soon as the supplier releases it. I learned the hard way how much this can really cost. It took me four months and ten pounds of my sweat to finally receive a freight claim for $85,000 when a truckload of plastic resin overturned in a dust storm outside Needles, CA. Had the shipment been FOB Delivered, it would have been the supplier's responsibility to file and negotiate the freight claim. Discount rates with common carriers today are in the 60% range. What is often done under a "Freight Prepaid and Billed" order is the supplier charges the customer for the full class rate and the discount from the carrier becomes profit.

Negotiating for timely delivery is mandatory. On-time delivery can save you considerable money when the cost of carrying inventory is considered. Having negotiated the timing of delivery, make sure you monitor it. It's also important to negotiate the mode of delivery. Surface shipments using their boat, truck or rail transportation are the first priority because they are normally the lowest in cost. If the delivery is late, negotiate with the supplier so that he pays the difference for more expensive transport, such as air freight, in order to meet your delivery requirements. JIT imposes stringent delivery requirements which must be negotiated up front.

QUANTITY

Negotiating seems to be simple. If I order 100 items, I expect 100 good items to be delivered. But we all know from experience that this does not always happen. If you've ever bought printed material, you know what I mean. One of the conventions in the printing industry is that "Overruns or underruns not to exceed 10% on quantities up to 10,000 ... shall constitute acceptable delivery. The printer will bill for actual quantity delivered within this tolerance."

If you need 10,000 labels to affix to 10,000 of your product, a shipment of 9,000 is going to leave you with 1,000 unlabeled items. A shipment of 11,000 will leave you with making payment on 1,000 labels you never used.

The lesson here is to watch for such conventions and monitor the quantity shipped to determine what the real tolerance is. You could wind up, over time, paying a lot for your supplier's inefficiencies. If, as a result of your monitoring, you find a supplier who consistently delivers the correct quantity (at the required level of quality and on time, 100% of the time), are you willing to reward the supplier during the next round of negotiations? This is one of the ways in which you can develop a better relationship.

I came up with some interesting data from three corrugated suppliers I was monitoring:

SUPPLIER	QUANTITY RANGE
A	+1 to +10
B	+4 to +10
C	+5 to +7

None of these suppliers undershipped or used the -10% which they said they needed. Supplier C actually was ±1% on a planned 6% overshipment. The corrugated industry has made some amazing progress through automation. They can now produce *exact* quantities and perform in-line changeovers in three seconds. Know your supplier's process, then you can negotiate from knowledge, instead of feelings.

Earlier, we said that long-term relationships with suppliers are desirable and should be the goal. However, you will have problems if you plan to manufacture 100,000 units over the next year and lock yourself into a contract with a supplier for exactly that amount. It's possible that, during the course of the year, the market may change and sales may increase or decrease dramatically. If, halfway through the contract period, you discover that you will sell only 75,000 units for the year, then you are still committed to raw material or components for 25,000 additional units for which you have no use. You can either try to sell it for scrap, lose money through cancellation charges or hold it as JIC (Just-In-Case) inventory.

Establish a window around the quantity. Be honest with your supplier. In the preceding example, the buyer should have approached the supplier and said, "We're forecasting as low as

75,000 units or as high as 150,000 units." Do this because you want to establish trust with your supplier. Let him know the window of possibility. In the contract, you can put in clauses saying that if only 75,000 units are purchased, the cost will be $1.00 each. If 100,000 units are bought, the rate will be $0.98 each. If 150,000 units are bought, the cost goes down to $0.95 each. Even though the quantity varies, you should still negotiate price up front, *not after the fact*.

SOLE AND SINGLE SOURCE SUPPLIER ISSUES

To gain the most advantage in planning your negotiation strategy, it is important to know as much as possible about your supplier. Start your evaluation process by determining whether your supplier is a sole or single source. Knowing the difference can significantly strengthen your bargaining powers.

A **sole source** is defined as follows:

> A sole supplier is one that is unique; literally, the one and only source in the cosmic universe who can supply the component you need to buy.

A **single source** is defined as follows:

> A single supplier is one particular source that you chose to buy from, although other supply avenues exist.

It would seem at first glance that you have very little leverage when dealing with a sole source because you can't readily obtain the material somewhere else. But don't give up the ship! That doesn't mean the possibility of negotiation ends. Remember, and remind the sole supplier, that you do represent some percentage of his business. Make them aware of the fact that you have three other alternatives open to you as well in order to gain leverage in the negotiations:

> 1. You could make the product yourself. Before you start saying that it's not feasible to make it yourself, remember that it is important that the supplier perceives it as a feasible alternative. You might want to request some quotes from his raw material suppliers to show that you are actively investigating the possibility.

> 2. Is there some other company that could help you gear up for the production of the item? If it is a sole source market, there is a good chance that there is room for more competition. Again, the supplier's perception of the power of your position is what you have working for you.

> 3. You could look at a redesign which would eliminate the need for the item you purchase from them. When was the last time your product was Value Analyzed? Working with our clients, we have seen the Total Manufactured Cost of products reduced by 1.5 to 22% during the first three months after establishing an employee involvement program to perform a Value Analysis on the products.

The second alternative may be very expensive, but the investment may be worth your money. A perfect situation for this alternative is a start-up company in need of some research and development money. By the time the start-up operation has grown, you will have already developed a good relationship with it. You will be able to get a good price on what used to be a sole source item. In fact, you gain in two ways — not only do you have a good rapport with one of the suppliers but now there is competition for the original sole source which should drive down his prices.

LOWERING COST THROUGH VALUE ENGINEERING, NOT NEGOTIATING

During the planning stage, it is very important to have a negotiated statement in writing which requires suppliers to conduct Value Engineering on a timely basis. Our objective is to constantly reduce the cost of the product. Value Engineering asks the following question:

What are we doing, and why are we doing it?

The following lists some of the considerations you will have to evaluate in a Value Engineering approach:

> **Reduce the cost of the product by:**
> Design change and simplification.
> Process changes.
> System changes.
> Early involvement.
> Shorten learning curve.

As a footnote, all Value Engineering must be accepted by design management as part of your team strategy.

CASE STUDY

Let's walk through an example of what we have been talking about. One of your suppliers is asking for a 13.3 percent price increase for a treated gasket they sell to you. You purchase approximately $350,000 worth of gaskets a year from this supplier. This represents 75 percent of all the gaskets you use and 12 percent of all the gaskets she produces. For the past thirty months, there has not been a single price increase.

You also purchase 25 percent of your gaskets from another supplier. Their gasket price is three times as much, but this company's product has a better record of preventing leaks.

Meanwhile, your 75 percent supplier has revised her processes to improve the leak integrity of the gasket and needs $78,000 for capital improvements. Since the seller's costs have increased 30 percent over the past 30 months, they claim that they are making no profit.

The supplier also claims that you should already be noticing the benefits of the quality improvement program and that their price is still below the competition's, even with a 13 percent increase. They blame the company's recent poor delivery record on suppliers who don't meet their deadlines.

You argue that nobody else is asking for such a large increase and quality and delivery are still below the levels at which they should be. The price increase will equal $46,550 more per year in expenditures for these gaskets.

What should you do in this situation?

SOLUTION

There are ten question or areas to address in planning for and executing a negotiation in this type of situation:

1. Make sure you are dealing with the right person.
2. Determine where the power is and define your situation — what are your strengths?
3. Look for a long-term relationship — how can you build one?
4. Determine the motivation of both the buyer and seller.
5. Establish your goals and objectives — min/max levels, MIL ranking.
6. Find out the product strategy — for how long will you need the product?
7. Begin trading information with the supplier.
8. Start making decisions — what are you going to accept and demand?
9. Identify customer restraints.
10. Quantify the actual cost of using leaky gaskets — service costs in the field, replacement costs, warranty cost, insurance claims from customers, lost customers.

One of the first things you should do is request an audit. Find out what their expenses are and what factors contribute to her costs. This audit may show that the company's expenses aren't as high as claimed or that the company's high costs are due to inefficiency. Make it clear that you have suffered some excess expenses because of the company's inconsistent delivery schedule and mediocre quality levels. In qualifying potential suppliers, all suppliers must undergo a financial analysis to see if they can perform for the long run.

It may be more cost beneficial to pay three times the price and buy all of the gaskets from the source currently getting 25% of your business. Develop a single source with this supplier of *quality* gaskets. The price differential may be far less than three times if they are your single source of choice. Quality first, then delivery and then price. Total Acquisition Cost, or life cycle costing, reveals some extremely important factors. Buying gaskets that leak when customers are involved lends credence to this statement:

Price is irrelevant.

What is my cost?

To begin to build trust, you can offer to work with her company in getting the sub-suppliers to improve their delivery record. Instead of bearing the burden of all the capital cost increases ($78,000), you might offer to bear only a percentage of these costs. Some form of price jump is inevitable if you do not include Value Analysis as part of the agreement.

In the meantime, examine alternate sources. Find out where your competition is buying gaskets of similar quality and how much they pay. Knowing more about alternate sources gives you the ability to take higher risks in the negotiations. As long as you know that you can get gaskets elsewhere, nobody can corner you into a 13 percent increase. An alternate source could be a company which would be willing to put the gasket you need into production. Even though this option may take six to nine months, it still gives you a bargaining chip.

In this example, I would also contact the 25 percent supplier whose gaskets cost three times as much. Find out if he would cut prices if you doubled your annual order. If your prime supplier refuses to concede on prices, you could cut your order by a full third and give the extra business to the other supplier. In this scenario, each supplier would be delivering half of your gasket order each year. In six to nine months, you can evaluate which gasket source is the most cost effective. In such a scenario, your prime supplier is in danger of losing everything. No supplier can afford to lose 12 percent of its business. Ideally, a supplier will see that it pays to work together to find a mutually acceptable price. Once friendly negotiations are taking place, both of you can begin working to reduce costs. Have your engineers review the supplier's process. See if there's an easy way to cut costs that hasn't been seen before.

TRAINING AND EDUCATION

My son, Mark, recently graduated from law school and passed the Florida bar, having already received an MBA. Although it cost over $100,000 for all that education, he never received more than three hours of training in negotiation. I'm sure he thinks that business is only concerned with Profit and Loss statements and balance sheets.

We must train our buyers and salespeople in the techniques of negotiation. At a recent class in negotiation which I was teaching for the National Association of Purchasing Management (NAPM),

---

"We must train our people
to negotiate now ...
in order to save dollars
tomorrow!"

I asked two questions of the thirty-two people present:

Question: How many years of purchasing experience do you have?

Answer: The average for the class was 4.5 years.

Question: How many of you have taken a negotiation course before?

Answer: Eight people, or twenty-five percent, had taken a course prior to our program.

We need to ask ourselves how much money has each company spent or left on the negotiating table because of a lack of training. It is our belief that every single buyer and salesperson should take a course once every two to five years and read a new negotiations book every year.

There is a difference between education and training. A colleague told me about his daughter who came home from school one day and said that tomorrow the teacher was going to give a class in sex education. The colleague said he would let her attend, but he said if the class was on sex training—*no way!*

THE GAME OF NEGOTIATION

Keep in mind that negotiation is something of a game. Make the other side comfortable by being the first to concede something. The supplier will now be more willing to work with you because you have shown good faith. With trust, the information can begin flowing. That is the name of the game.

SUGGESTIONS

1. Review an upcoming situation in which you will be attempting to negotiate an agreement or solution. Maintain a balance between trust and cooperation.

2. List the obstacles which will keep you from achieving a win/win solution.

3. Select a situation in the future where you would like to develop a win/win approach. List what you expect and what you expect from the other party. Approach the other party to determine if there is an interest in pursuing a win/win approach.

4. Review your negotiation style to see if you are able to convert to a win/win paradigm.

5. Develop a win/win model to be followed by each Purchasing person.

CHAPTER FIVE

"You can get anything you want, once you realize that you are always negotiating."

TYPES OF NEGOTIATIONS

FINDING THE BEST DEAL

In an age where concepts are becoming the norm, the role of negotiation is changing dramatically. Previously, many companies have viewed purchasing's job as mainly clerical, a job in which orders were placed. Today, companies must realize that there needs to be a new emphasis on purchasing management since material content is over 50 percent of product cost.

Knowledgeable purchasers know that it is their obligation to get the best deal for the company in terms of quality, delivery and total cost. Awareness of the bottom line is vital in order for the company to make a profit.

OBSTACLES

It is a sound idea to control all purchasing activities within a function or under one person's authority. We want to avoid situations in which non-purchasing professionals negotiate with suppliers for components or services. If this is allowed to occur, the result is usually bad for the company and for the individual. When someone other than a Purchasing professional negotiates a purchase, there is room for graft and corruption because of the seller's zest to sell at any cost.

The areas most susceptible to graft and fraud within a company are Engineering, Traffic and Purchasing. As a purchaser, it's important to make certain that you have a handle on all aspects of buying — from negotiation to delivery.

A recent article in the *Palm Beach Post*, "Sex sells at business conventions — routinely," deals with indiscretions in corporate America today. Many suppliers will provide prostitutes to buyers who attend conventions, junkets, seminars and sales meetings. One company, Hewlett-Packard, has moved to eliminate this and similar practices by issuing a 15-page ethics policy which, in part, says:

> "Advertising novelties, favors, or entertainment may only be given to customers and suppliers at HP expense if: a) they are consistent with accepted business practice; b) they are of limited value and cannot be construed as a bribe or payoff; c) they do not violate any law, government regulation or generally accepted ethical standards, and d) public disclosure of the facts will not embarrass HP."

Despite such policies on ethics, many female executives who were surveyed are not convinced that the mixing of sex and business will come to an end. They believe it will be particularly difficult to end such practices when U.S. companies deal with foreign companies and salespeople. Many international sales personnel expect an escort when they arrive in a foreign country. This will present significant problems as more and more women move into negotiating roles. Other women, however, feel that the mixing of sex and business will diminish as younger men start taking over the positions of older men who may expect gratuities and other such services. One female manager reports that in her past year of business travel, she dealt with men in their thirties who were interested in negotiating for her company's products and nothing more.

UTILIZING DISTRIBUTORS

The most direct method for purchasing products is to buy from the manufacturer. Buying a product from a distributor increases your price, but it may lower your total cost. The distributor requires a profit in exchange for storage, service and transportation costs. In order to purchase directly from a manufacturer, you normally are required to order large volumes. Therefore, small buyers will most likely utilize a distribution center.

Future Electronics, a Massachusetts firm, has started a World Class program for distribution in which their customers can do one-stop shopping. The company's objective is to negotiate a win/win arrangement whereby their customers can purchase 100 percent of their electronic components from Future. In exchange, Future will supply kits of material as required (Just-In-Time).

A company with multiple divisions in different states should take advantage of the buying power of all its divisions by negotiating in aggregate. A single division negotiating a purchase on its own has only a portion of the volume that the whole company has. Together, the team can negotiate better prices and terms. In the case of a decentralized company where each division or plant works independently, the purchaser in the plant with the highest volume should provide a lead negotiator for that commodity and let others feed off that arrangement.

TRAINING FOR THE NEGOTIATION

The most important part of negotiation occurs long before you sit down at the bargaining table. Most negotiation books don't deal with preparation and planning. It is the responsibility of Purchasing to coordinate with all personnel prior to a negotiating session. People must be trained in what to say and how to say it to the supplier. It's important for people to understand what tactics will be used if they are present during negotiations. A buyers' entire effort can be lost by someone else in the organization tipping his or her hand.

If an engineer blurts out how badly a certain commodity is required, then the supplier knows he has the upper hand. If someone admits that Supplier A is the only usable source for a particular item, then the buyer loses the edge and the company loses money. Make certain that all the players know what's going on and what other departments are doing.

VALUE OF NEGOTIATING

Most professional buyers spend less than 20 percent of their time on negotiations. We believe buyers should spend a minimum of 50 percent of their time on negotiations. As we have repeatedly said, negotiation entails not only the bargaining phase, but planning, information gathering, research, timing, deadlines and contract writing. A buyer who understands the entire negotiation process will save a company money.

Good buyers or purchasing agents should save their company ten times their salary each year. While company CEOs are starting to recognize the importance of the purchasing function, many managers still tend to look at purchasers as order placers. As a result, managers, who are frequently the ones that generate requirements, don't work with the purchasing department in negotiating good deals with a supplier. It's clear then that part of a company's task is to educate its people about negotiating in order to show them that savings are lost if there is no cooperation from all departments.

USING YOUR THIRD PARTY EFFECTIVELY

A company must establish a negotiating program where results are rewarded. If a buyer/negotiator brings a third party into a negotiation session, the supplier normally talks to the boss. In this case, the purchaser loses credibility as the power transfers to the boss. The buyer must have authority. It is up to the boss to refer questions to the buyer. When a third party is utilized for negotiating an agreement, the purchaser must have previously established the ground rules prior to the entry of the party. Let us provide you with a recent example.

Theresa, our client service representative, wanted to buy a new Toyota. In the previous two weeks, she had shopped at all the area dealers. She finally settled on a particular model that she could afford at a dealer where she believed she could make the best deal.

She set up an appointment to purchase the car on the last Saturday morning of the month. I'm sure the salesperson expected only her to arrive, but both myself and Jerry Claunch went with her to help and to sharpen our skills.

The first thing we did was to ask that the "invisible" sales manager be present. You know, the person the salesperson goes to every ten minutes to see if the deal is okay. In addition, we wanted the credit manager to be present so that there would be no surprises about long-term service contracts, credit terms, points or anything else.

What they didn't know was that Theresa had already prequalified for a loan at a local bank prior to our meeting and that she intended to finance her purchase wherever the best deal could be made. In other words, we were looking at Total Cost.

That done, we proceeded to sit on a couch in the middle of the showroom instead of in one of those little offices, much to the dismay of the sales group. All the time that our negotiating process was going on, other buyers in the showroom stood close by to see what was going on. The sales group was trying to move us to close quickly, but we were in no hurry. The process took four hours before we finally did close.

Each of us had a role to play in the negotiations as well. Theresa — I just want a car. Jerry — There must be a better deal. Me — The Bad Guy. Since we knew that time is important to commission sales, we intended to tie up as many people as we could, for as long as we could. To make a long story short, Theresa purchased the car for $100 over Dealer Invoice price, with no financing and with a long-term warranty, registration and title included. She also drove the car home that day with dealer plates.

BUYING A HOME

Buying a home to live or invest in requires skills normally not used. Emotions often play a large role. Let's review the purchase of a residence to show how to keep them under control.

In the typical scenario in which you and a significant other purchase a home, there are more people involved than you may at first imagine. There are two buyers, two sellers, a real estate agent for each side and a lawyer for each side. In addition, don't forget the bank or mortgage company's representative. What was thought to be a simple process now involves the following people:

> **2 Buyers**
> **2 Sellers**
> **2 Real estate agents**
> **2 Lawyers**
> <u>**1 Bank representative**</u>
> **9 People**

As buyers, you have the money and everybody else wants to take it away from you. Your money will pay real estate commissions, lawyer fees and closing costs.

Let's look at a simple purchase. A seller offers a house for sale through a multiple listing service for $149,900 — they never seem to ask $150,000. Your task is to find out what the seller will really take for the bottom line. So you ask some questions:

> **How long have you owned the house?**
> **Why do you want to sell it?**
> **How long has it been on the market?**

Does it include (certain items)?
How much is left on the mortgage?
Is the mortgage assumable?
When can we take possession?

One mistake that many inexperienced people make is to find all the faults with the property. When you state all the things wrong with my *home*, I will get defensive. Remember that a person's home is their castle.

The approach we like to take is to point out all the positive things as we go along and keep track of the negative items on a separate document. From these questions and surveys, you then determine what you think the seller will accept and how much you think you can afford.

When buying a home, it is very important to treat it as a short-term purchase. The average person turns a house over long before the mortgage is paid in full. If we keep this idea in mind, we will be able to walk away from a deal we don't like.

Remember the story of Donald Trump's purchase of MAR-LAR-GO. He initially offered a figure that was refused. About a year later, the owners of the property approached him. His new offer was significantly lower than his first offer. We all know the end of the story; he owns the property. Had he taken the approach that I must have this property, he would have paid more for it.

Buying a home is not a win/win situation. It is highly unlikely that you will buy another home from the same seller. Our approach is to get the lowest offer possible. The seller will not sell if he doesn't feel the offer is acceptable.

FREQUENCY OF CONTACT

Typically, buyers will only see suppliers with whom they are presently doing business or with whom they are having problems. Buyers can get complacent with their present suppliers because buyers often do not have enough time to perform negotiations because of a heavy work load. To build a high level of trust, it is necessary to keep in contact, based on a procurement plan, with all suppliers.

As a minimum, we recommend that buyers visit their major suppliers at least two times annually. It is extremely important to establish a relationship with the supplier's manufacturing facility. Otherwise, when you tell a salesperson that there is a problem, he or she will just contact the factory for a resolution of your problem. You need to have continuous contact with people at each supplier's plant who can continue to work toward reducing cost and can solve business issues.

ISSUES

One of the keys to negotiation is managing the many variables. A supplier who knows he has trapped you into a deal because he is the only available supplier is able to drive a very hard bargain. When buyers are against the wall, with little lead-time and only one possible supplier, they have to know the options.

NEGOTIATING FOR QUALITY

Either you or your purchasing department, in order to be an effective negotiator, must also educate suppliers about the level of quality which your company expects in order for them to meet certification guidelines. Your production process will suffer as a result of low quality at each supplier's plant. A policy is required when you receive defective parts. A rejection form should be completed and sent back to each supplier with the rejected lot. Maintain a copy of every instance in a file.

Then, when it's time to negotiate, pull out the copies of the rejection forms and ask what has been done to improve the process which caused these errors. The supplier must demonstrate that improvements have been made. It costs less for quality parts.

It should be clear to suppliers that you will not tolerate token efforts at delivery and quality. The buyer's power is in demanding that each supplier knows that quality is the main issue. The more you emphasize it, the more the supplier will work to meet customer specifications. The buyer is ultimately responsible for the quality of the items ordered. Don't let people shirk this responsibility. Handle each problem with quality as it occurs.

PHONE NEGOTIATIONS

Although phone negotiations are generally shorter in duration and involve smaller sums of money, they do alter bargaining. You should be aware that the phone offers opportunities as well as disadvantages. You can use the phone, for example, to control timing in negotiations. If you don't want to talk at any particular time, you don't need to take the call. Or, if the negotiations aren't going well, you can claim a bad connection or cut things short due to some other interruption in your office. They even have a gadget on the market now which creates the sounds of static, phone ringing or paging. In phone negotiations, you have a built-in buffer which can give you the edge.

On the other hand, because there is no visual contact whereby you can read facial expressions and body language, using the phone can lead to misunderstandings such as making unwarranted assumptions or failing to address the other person's needs. These errors often occur because negotiators usually fail to prepare as thoroughly as they would for face to face negotiations. They also occur because it is easy to assume something is understood. This assumption could be fatal. Never assume that anything is understood. A good way to avoid this situation is to ask the other person to explain himself, to repeat what he means or what he thinks you have told him. Try to be more precise yourself in the words you choose and, above all, listen much more carefully. We often follow up a phone call with a letter of confirmation.

Another way to lessen the chances of confusion is to approach phone negotiations with careful preparation. Make a list of specific issues in advance and know what your tolerance acceptance levels are. Make sure you don't leave anything out by trying a dry run. Go through the upcoming phone conversation in your mind and try to anticipate all the contingencies. Adopt the motto of the Boy Scouts and "Be Prepared!" Misunderstandings are all to often at the root of badly negotiated deals, lawsuits and downed production lines.

MORE TACTICS TO WATCH OUT FOR

Many people view negotiations as a competitive process and expect only grudging cooperation. Although some negotiators may claim to be cooperative, you can see their combativeness in their mannerisms, style, choice of words and body language. Try to avoid dealing with a person who is faking cooperation and not ready to negotiate.

When a supplier comes back to negotiate a deal that has gone bad for him, the buyer should be willing to listen and cooperate. This is not to say that the buyer should concede necessary terms of the agreement, but that he should develop a better relationship by agreeing to rework the deal. This sets up a positive atmosphere for the future.

Don't be naive in renegotiation. Be truthful. Tell suppliers that you are willing to help solve issues with them. You may allow them to charge a slightly higher rate. Then notify them that they run the risk of losing credibility and probably the contract.

HAGGLING

Negotiation happens everywhere. It's not limited to bargaining on the cost of parts or material. It can also happen in the service industries or in retail stores.

For example, it is usually better to bargain with a store owner from Monday through Thursday. Weekends are busy and the merchant doesn't have to sell to you. There are other customers coming in the door all day. Also, try asking for a discount if you pay with cash. Many stores will also match the prices of competitors if you show them an advertisement.

Even the cost of surgery is negotiable. Get estimates from a number of reputable surgeons. If you have a favorite doctor, ask him or her to match the best price. The same principle holds true for repairs on appliances or cars. Get more than one estimate and ask for references.

On a recent trip to the West Coast, one of us, Pete, forgot to take along a pair of black shoes. He decided upon arriving that he would go to a mall and buy a pair. He was pleasantly surprised to find that there were several shoe stores in the mall.

I selected a store that sold the top brand of men's shoes and proceeded to spend time looking at what they had to offer. In a short while, the sales clerk asked if I needed any help. I told him that he could start by showing me everything he had in a size nine. The look on the salesperson's face was priceless.

"You want to try on every shoe in size nine?" he asked.

"Just the black ones," I reassured him.

After about an hour of trying on shoes, I settled for a black pair, size nine, for $130. Then I asked for my discount. The poor clerk went into shock.

"I'm sorry, sir," he said, "we don't discount in this store. But I could throw in a can of polish."

I proceeded to ask him what type of polish and how big of a can and what about shoe trees and, by the way, what if I buy two pairs. Maybe, I told him, you could show me the burgundy shoes and then the brown ones.

The result of all this negotiating was that I bought two pairs of shoes (one burgundy and one black) at a 10 percent discount with two pairs of shoe trees, two pairs of socks and two cans of polish thrown in to get me out of the store so the clerk could start selling to other customers. Who said the best stores don't discount? You need *patience*!

SALES NEGOTIATING

Buying is the flip side of selling and negotiation is needed while doing both. That is why we need to look at purchasing agents and buyers as more than paper shufflers. They need to be aware of a myriad of internal and external factors in order to do their work effectively. As we have already shown, production, quality engineering and total cost considerations are all essential parts of the negotiation process. Buyers should be aware of certain strategies that sellers use during negotiations. The following list identifies some of these tactics:

- **Waiting it out — Seller waits to the last possible moment to negotiate.**

- **Down the middle — Seller's initial offer comes in below expectations of buyer in order to meet half way.**

- **That's the way it's done — Seller tells buyer that this is the way business is done in the industry.**

- **Pasta approach — Seller links best deal to buyer agreeing on other deals.**

- **That's it — Seller tells buyer that they don't negotiate. Take it or leave it.**

- **Just one more thing — Seller appears to give buyer all the information he needs, but at the last moment, he always brings in something he forgot to discuss earlier.**

Learn to recognize these tactics so that they are not used against you in the course of your negotiations.

LABOR NEGOTIATING

Labor negotiations often results in no more than labor threatening to strike and management threatening to close, relocate or lock out workers. Such seems to be the case in the negotiations which

- **Continuous negotiation — Create a team of management and labor which sits down and discusses disagreements before they become major crises.**

- **Cut and divide — Take a large issue and divide it into smaller issues which can be dealt with by various committees.**

- **Ounce of prevention — If a crisis seems imminent, ask all sides to get together before tempers reach the breaking point.**

- **One for all, all for one — Bargain openly with all the unions present so that everybody knows how the company's resources are being spread about.**

- **Separate wheat from chaff — Negotiate non-economic aspects independently from wages, etc.**

- **Early bird — Start negotiating a new contract far in advance of any deadline so that pressure will not mount.**

surrounded the fate of the *New York Post.* The publisher was about to announce the end of the newspaper when labor negotiators and the Mayor Dinkins of New York stopped him and asked him to start renegotiating. There are other alternatives to this type of negotiating with labor. We suggest the alternatives on the preceeding page.

Once again, the aim of negotiation, even in a labor setting, is to create a partnership. Labor negotiating can be a win/win proposition for both sides.

MODES OF NEGOTIATION

Planning— Negotiation is an ongoing process in which the communication of information that is necessary to plan effective strategies is openly shared.

Cooperative— There is always a better deal if you take time to build a relationship in which all parties work to make the pie bigger.

Competitive — This is a method of negotiation in which neither party is willing to focus on the issues and ignore the peripherals. It usually takes the "I win, you lose" approach.

Quick Deal — Often the result of competitive negotiation, a quick deal usually has an adverse impact on future negotiations.

Phone Negotiations — This type of negotiation has its advantages and drawbacks. The key is to approach phone negotiations with careful preparation and without any rush. You can always call back. It is better to be the initiator than the receiver.

Collaborative — This mode requires close coordination between Quality Assurance, Purchasing, suppliers and customers as the foundation for a partnership. It's demonstrated by a willingness to work together.

Conflicts — There should be an accurate and responsive corrective action system to generate the correct requirements for customers and suppliers. This avoids the firefighting, crisis management approach which is often used during conflicts.

Attitudinal — The right attitude is critical. Develop an attitude of trust and cooperation. If the right attitude is not developed, then adversarial positioning is likely to occur.

Organizational — During the process of negotiation, the different departments within a company must work in harmony and share information. No department should ever act without the approval of the negotiating team. You need a company-wide strategic plan for negotiations.

Personal — In this mode, you should take a positive view and practice your skills both internally and externally. You must also avoid taking what happens in negotiations personally. Don't ever make personal attacks on another person either.

Partnership — With training and planning, anybody can fashion and close deals which satisfy the needs and wants of all parties.

WIN/WIN SALARY STRATEGY

Who is the worst person to negotiate for? You are. Many people view the negotiation process as bargaining or haggling. This thought process is negative. A positive approach would entail practicing your negotiating skills daily both internally and externally. We're sure that Red Sox star pitcher Roger Clemens was positive about his value when he and his agent recently negotiated a four-year contract for $21.5 million.

Suppose you were never happy with your salary reviews in the past and want to be involved in negotiating a better salary in the future. I'm sure that every reader wonders how the percent of increase was derived. We know we never found how to get a 20 percent increase.

Instead of going in and making a demand, we think each person should follow the same philosophy that we wrote about earlier. In the case of asking for a salary increase, we recommend that four steps be taken.

1. Present your employer with data showing success in the past to support your claims.

2. Provide fair but difficult goals and objectives for the next twelve months. Hook the percent of increase to achieving these goals and objectives.

3. Verify what the competition is receiving for the same task. This can be obtained from Personnel or professional societies.

4. Establish quarterly reviews for progress against objectives.

You are then a part of a win/win structure concerning your future.

Keep the following characteristics in mind to reinforce this structure:

CHARACTERISTICS OF A SUCCESSFUL SALARY NEGOTIATION

- **State the goals initially.**
- **Learn about the company's goals.**
- **Gather data and information.**
- **Arrive at a compromise.**
- **Communicate frequently.**

It is extremely important to state what you want up front. People tend to assume (ass/u/me) that they know what the other party will not tell them. It is extremely dangerous to assume in negotiation. When in doubt, ask! Our intent is to build bridges, not burn them. Roger Dawson says, "You can get anything you want, but you got to do more than ask." How true that is.

People find it hard to negotiate for themselves because they cannot be objective when they feel emotional attachment. In preparation for negotiating for yourself, review what you consider to be the facts with a friend who is not involved in the situation. Ask a friend to point out the areas you may not be looking at objectively and the ones to which you seem to have the most emotional attachment. Then ask your friend to participate in a mock negotiation. Have the friend assume your role and you take the role of the person you will be negotiating with. Don't be surprised if you're not that happy with they way your friend plays your role. He or she may be doing you the biggest favor possible by playing you the way you appear. This mock negotiation also gives you the opportunity to see the process from the other side's perspective. The experience can prove to be a way to help you become more objective and better control your emotions.

NEGOTIATING A DIVORCE

Equally emotional is negotiating a divorce. There are many techniques we recommend. Some people want to pursue the approach of getting all you can and literally screwing the other person as much as possible. Others want to achieve a 50/50 split. Depending on the past relationship and what triggered the split has a lot to do with what method will be employed.

Even in the best of situations where one party hires a lawyer, the other side has no choice but to hire one, too. This could turn the divorce into the most frustrating negotiation you have ever been involved in. The court and both lawyers are in it for the money. They are not there to help because they feel sorry for you. Their task is to get as much money from you as they can.

Each side will request so much paperwork that it will take months to unravel. You are not allowed to have any control in scheduling the dates of various hearings. All offers go through a third party (one lawyer to the other). When you try a direct approach, the response is: "In your best interest, I advise you not to sign or do this." We must learn to manage the people we are paying. Remember that the lawyer works for you; you don't work for them.

A recent example from a friend comes to mind. He offered his ex-spouse a very good offer early in the process. Her lawyer felt that it was to good to be true and that he must be trying to hide something, so he told her to wait until he could review the whole case. When this case finally got settled, the results were far less than the first offer. Even in community property states, each side does not present a worst or best case. What is required, we think, is a system that allows negotiation to take place so that a win/win result can be had for both parties.

Divorce negotiation is always difficult because it violates the first rule of negotiating: Don't get emotionally involved! Since this relationship was once a partnership and is now being dissolved, people forget that the process still requires communication.

RATING YOURSELF AS A NEGOTIATOR

We have prepared a list of 25 questions which you can review in order to ascertain your current negotiating style. The key is to answer the question as you are today, not as what you would like to be. This will better enable you to identify the areas which need improvement.

1. **Do you generally go into negotiations well prepared?**

   a) Majority of the time.
   b) Often.
   c) Sometimes.
   d) Not frequently.
   e) Play it by ear.

2. **Do you believe what you are told in negotiations?**

   a) No, I'm very skeptical.
   b) Moderately skeptical.
   c) Sometimes unbelieving.
   d) Generally trusting.
   e) Almost always believing.

3.   To what extent is it important for you to be liked?

   a) Extremely important.
   b) Very important.
   c) Important.
   d) Not too important.
   e) Doesn't make any difference.

4.   How do you appear in negotiations?

   a) Highly competitive.
   b) Mostly competitive, but a good part cooperative.
   c) Mostly cooperative, but a good part competitive.
   d) Very cooperative.
   e) About half and half.

5.   When a deal you made turns out to be quite bad for the other party, do you let them renegotiate a better deal?

   a) Willing to listen.
   b) Sometimes, based on situation.
   c) Reluctantly.
   d) Hardly ever — they made the deal.
   e) It's their problem.

6.   Do you have a tendency to be threatened?

   a) Frequently threatened.
   b) Numerous occasions.
   c) Occasionally.
   d) Infrequently.
   e) Very infrequently.

7.   **Are you a good listener?**

a) Excellent.
b) Better than most, good.
c) Average.
d) Below average.
e) Poor listener.

8.   **How thoroughly do you negotiate or develop a strategy for priorities with people in your own organization?**

a) Very well.
b) Not very often.
c) Negotiate often, hard and well.
d) Negotiate sometimes.
e) Generally do what is required and expected.

9.   **How would you feel about negotiating a 10 percent raise when the average department raise is 5 percent?**

a) Would avoid it.
b) Would make a pass at it reluctantly.
c) Would do it with a little apprehension.
d) Not afraid to try it.
e) Would enjoy the experience.

10.   **Do you think clearly under pressure?**

a) Yes, very well.
b) Better than most people.
c) About average.
d) Below average
e) Not well at all.

11.   To what extent is it important for you to be respected?

a) Extremely important.
b) Very important.
c) Important.
d) Not too important.
e) Doesn't make any difference.

12.   Are you an open-minded person?

a) Yes, very much so.
b) Better than most.
c) Most of the time.
d) Somewhat closed-minded.
e) Pretty fixed in my ways.

13.   How important do you consider integrity?

a) Extremely important.
b) Very important.
c) Important.
d) Somewhat important.
e) It's a tough world.

14.   When you have the power, do you use it?

a) Yes, to the extent I can.
b) I use it without any guilt feelings.
c) I use it in behalf of justice as I see justice.
d) I don't like to use it.
e) I take it easy on the other person.

15. **How sensitive are you to other people's wants?**

a) Highly sensitive.
b) Very sensitive.
c) Sometimes sensitive.
d) Less sensitive than most people.
e) Not sensitive at all.

16. **How do you feel about getting personally involved with the other party?**

a) I avoid it completely.
b) I'm quite comfortable.
c) Not bad; not good.
d) I'm attracted to getting close.
e) I go out of my way to get close.

17. **What kind of targets or goals do you tend to set?**

a) Hard to reach targets.
b) Quite hard to reach.
c) Not too hard; not too easy.
d) Targets of modest range.
e) Relatively easy targets.

18. **Are you a patient negotiator?**

a) Yes, very patient.
b) More than most.
c) Average.
d) Below average.
e) I get it over with. What's the point of fooling around?

19. **Are you persistent in negotiation?**

   a) Extremely persistent.
   b) Very persistent.
   c) Fairly persistent.
   d) Not very persistent.
   e) Not persistent at all.

20. **How sensitive are you to the personal issues facing the opponent in negotiation? (The non-business issues like job security, work load, getting along with the boss, vacation, not rocking the boat.)**

   a) Very sensitive.
   b) Concerned.
   c) Average sensitivity.
   d) Not too sensitive.
   e) Hardly sensitive at all.

21. **How committed are you to the opponent's satisfaction?**

   a) Very committed. I try for win/win.
   b) Somewhat committed.
   c) Neutral, but I hope they don't get hurt.
   d) I'm a bit concerned.
   e) It's everybody for themselves.

22. **Do you tend to emphasize the limits of your power?**

   a) Yes, very much so.
   b) Usually more than I like to.

c) I weigh it.
d) I don't dwell on it
e) I mostly think positively.

23. **Do you study the limits of the other person's power?**

a) Yes, most of the time
b) Quite a bit.
c) I weigh their power.
d) It's hard to appraise.
e) I let things develop at the session.

24. **How do you usually give in?**

a) Very slowly, if at all.
b) Moderately slowly.
c) About the same pace they do.
d) I try to move it along a little faster by giving more.
e) I don't mind giving hefty chunks and getting to the point.

25. **How would you feel if you had to say "I don't understand that" four times after four good explanations?**

a) Terrible, I wouldn't do it.
b) Quite embarrassed.
c) Would feel awkward.
d) Would do it without feeling too badly.
e) Wouldn't hesitate.

After you have completed these questions, compare your answers to those which appear on page 232. Allow four points for each answer. If you scored 64 or better, we consider your openness an advantage in developing a partnership for the long-term. A score below 60 requires significant work in order to be able to compete effectively in this area.

SCORE

84-100	**Excellent negotiator.**
64-80	**Good negotiator.**
44-60	**Average negotiator.**
24-40	**Poor negotiator.**
0-20	**Set in your ways.**

CHAPTER SIX

"An obstacle is not an end — it is a new beginning."

PRACTICAL
NEGOTIATING
TACTICS

I DON'T UNDERSTAND

A few years ago, I was negotiating with a prominent corporation in Japan. We arrived there on Saturday, rested on Sunday and started negotiations on Monday morning with a fresh outlook. We were going merrily along when we finally got to the discussions on quality. I made a very simple statement about what level of quality our company requires. Each of our suppliers must subscribe to our zero-defects policy. Within the next three years, we expect our supplier to achieve Six Sigma which translates into catching defects 99.9999998 percent of the time.

In response to our request, we were handed a quality manual which made the New York "Yellow Pages" look like a pamphlet.

"This is our quality manual," my negotiating partner informed me. "Everything you need to know is in here."

I looked at him as I tried to lift the manual up off the table and said, "I can't read all this in the time I'm here. Would you mind defining what we need to know?"

"Well," the supplier's representative said, "we use an AQL system here."

"I'm sorry," I said. "I don't understand what AQL is. I'm just a procurement person. Can you explain this concept of AQL to us?"

Keep in mind that the best strategy to utilize when negotiating with the Japanese or other foreign suppliers is the strategy which employs the "Why?" question. When everybody thinks that the issue is understood, ask one more question. Carefully search for and appraise pressure points.

My opposite anxiously agrees to explain AQL to me. He takes fifteen minutes, speaking part of the time in Japanese with his group and part of the time in English to us. When he is finished, I say, "I'm really very sorry, but I still don't understand. Can you please tell me one more time how that concept of AQL gets good parts?"

If, at this point, we were to reach an impasse, our strategy was to call a recess or schedule another meeting.

As for my question, it is an example of a common negotiating tactic — I didn't hear what I wanted to hear, so tell me one more time.

My negotiating partner then turned to another person at the table and asked him to go through an explanation of AQL once again so I could understand. By now, everybody is getting a little flustered because all the other details of this multimillion-dollar contract have been worked out. The new explainer spoke very slowly and only in English. When he finished, I got up and said, "Now, I understand what you're talking about. If you send me a lot of 100 parts and two parts are bad, I have to accept the lot."

They breathed a sigh of relief. "Yes, that's it," they told me.

"Well then," I responded, "I have a very simple solution to this problem. Why don't you just send me the 98 good ones and you keep the two bad ones for yourself."

The negotiating went on for a good while longer after that, but we achieved our zero-defects objective. I knew that they were quite capable of delivering zero-defect parts, but they thought that we would accept a 2% AQL because that was the prevailing U.S. standard and typical acceptance level for the type of component we were purchasing.

Never hesitate to say "I don't understand" numerous times. You won't lose any power or authority. In fact, saying those three words will help you in two ways. First, it is useful to play dumb when your negotiating opponent makes a statement or offer which is contrary to what you want. When you say, "I don't understand," you are sending a clear message to the other side: You are not saying what I want to hear. Eventually the other side will alter their statement just to get a different reaction. The revised statement may well be closer to what you want to hear. It is very likely that additional information will be given in the new explanation.

The second reason to say, "I don't understand," is because you really don't understand. The other negotiating side may be unclear or not know precisely what they are talking about. Don't let them be vague. Wait or force them to make a concise statement, a statement whose implications you fully understand or can accept. Anytime you think you can influence the other party, keep in mind a statement from The Cockle Bar: "Try ordering around someone else's dog."

Sir Robert Oppenheimer stated that "When you want something from a person, think first of what you can give him in return. Let him think it's he who is coming off best. But all the time make sure it is you in the end."

LISTENING TECHNIQUES

One of the most powerful negotiation tactics is to listen and be silent. Let the other side do all the talking. In the example above, I forced all the conversation to the other side. Many people feel they are losing control when the other party dominates the conversation. They think that they can improve their position by talking and explaining. But a negotiator who realizes that quiet rooms make people nervous has actually gained a considerable amount of power. When two people are in a room and one of them has the self-control to keep quiet, that person will learn a great deal. The other person will tend to talk more to fill the void. Let the other person talk and then ask more questions about a concept. Normally, the other party is willing to talk more and, in doing so, reveals valuable information. This can only help your position to achieve the plan established for this negotiating session.

On that same trip to the Bahamas with a group of business

associates, we entered the straw market. One of our group began to bargain with a basket maker in the booths at the very front of the market area. Other members of our group headed to the far corners in order to search for the basket weavers who had the time both to make the baskets and to sell them. The shops in the front of the market had time only to sell.

The best deal was made with the lady in the rear of the market. Our tactic was to use the prices from the front booths with the people in the rear of the market. We told what we wanted to pay and didn't say another word. The woman wanted the sale badly and kept making offers to which we simply nodded our heads. Eventually, we got the price we sought. Also, realize that the woman would not have sold anything to us, if she wasn't making a profit.

Listening also means asking questions, *not making statements*. This tactic must be practiced continuously to get the required results. When the situation warrants, you should go into the negotiation with a written list of questions to ask. If you are busy thinking of questions during negotiation, you will not be listening.

"Looking at bargains from a purely commercial point of view, someone is always cheated. But, looked at with the simple eye, both seller and buyer always win." This statement by David Grayson has significant merit in this type of negotiation. The merchant will not sell if she doesn't make a profit. Our goal was to arrive at that number.

SMOKE SCREENS

Another negotiating tactic with which you should be familiar is the one where the other side clouds the air with trivial and unimportant issues. At times, you may need to take this approach in order to strengthen your position. But when somebody uses it on you, retaliate by keeping your major issues on the table. Sometimes you just have to set the other party straight. Tell them that you can see exactly what they are trying to do and that it is a waste of time. Then get back to the issues that you have decided are important and deal with them.

Don't retreat by trying to defend your position. Make your statement, put your facts on the table and then let the other negotiator talk. Make them tell you why certain things should be done. Once your position is known, become a listener who deals with only the major issues.

A good example of this occurred at a negotiating session in which the other side's superiors did not show up. The people present suggested that we start the meeting and do what we could until the vice president of sales showed up. Imagine their shock when we informed them that we were leaving since the person who could sign the order was not present. It was remarkable what our ploy accomplished. Within five minutes, the vice president appeared.

From this experience we learned that the first question to ask is this:

> ## "Can everyone present sign,
>
> ## if an agreement is reached?"

Remember that when two sides work together, the result is that you win together. We can only reach a clear goal when all efforts are coordinated.

CONTROLLING THE PROCESS

Never quickly concede a position of power or control in a negotiating session. You aren't always in as weak a position as you imagine. When a supplier gives you a firm offer, the best reply is to say, "Let me think about it." You might find that this supplier, in a rush to fill quotas, will come down in price right away. The job of the supplier's salespeople is to bring in orders. They have to meet quotas and deadlines. Consequently, it is to your advantage to gain knowledge of their objectives.

Another power tactic to watch out for is the "good guy/bad guy" routine. The supplier's boss comes in with a sour face and makes negative comments about the potential deal. Even though this trick is as old as the hills, it still works today into forcing you to make concessions for fear of losing the deal. Don't let this tactic rattle you. If you see it happening, smile and say, "You aren't going to play good guy, bad guy with me, are you?"

Power negotiators always make sure the other side "wins." An attorney friend of mine dreamed up twenty-three paragraphs of requests one day to present to the other side. Some were absolutely ridiculous. He was sure that half of them would be thrown out immediately. What happened? The other side objected to one sentence in one paragraph. What did my friend do? He held out for two days before he reluctantly agreed to change it. The other side felt like they had won a major concession.

Peter Baron reminded us of a negotiation that Peter Grieco did for Texas Instruments. The company was battling with Commodore to gain a better position for the TI 99-4A home computer. Commodore was continuing to reduce their selling price which was forcing TI to keep pace. Bill Turner, now the President of ADP, hired one of us, Pete, to manage the material world of Texas Instruments Consumer Product Group of which Turner was then president.

Based on a simple A, B, C Pareto rating of supplier components, we discovered that the keyboard was one of the major "A" items. TI was using seven suppliers to manufacture the keyboard at an average price of $21 each. The first question we asked was "Why seven?" Our volume was 365,000 computers per month.

We put together a negotiation plan to reduce the supplier base to two or three companies in order to gain an advantage based on learning curves. The first objective was to invite all seven suppliers to bid on the job of being one of the three we would utilize. Bill Turner wanted to test my ability to lower the cost and provide marketing with a cost advantage on the selling price. He made a bet to take me out to dinner at the restaurant of my choice if I succeeded.

My tactic was to present a signed purchase order to each of the suppliers with all approvals. The purchase order was for 1,000,000 pieces for a total of $10,000,000. All that was missing was their name on the top. Two of the seven suppliers went for the carrot. One of them, a Japanese supplier, was so excited by the size of the order that they forgot to figure out the unit price. A third supplier negotiated a $13.50 price. The final result was that we eliminated four suppliers and lowered the price significantly.

GAINING POWER

In order to gain power in negotiation, you need to incorporate the following activities into your course of action:

Competitive knowledge — Conduct research about your competitor. Know what you can offer. A buyer's awareness of a supplier's production process is critical to successful negotiation. You need to identify suppliers who are best able to meet your requirements and who can deliver 100% quality on time, 100% of the time.

Legitimacy of an offer — Don't respond to offers which are clearly made in order to force you to show your hand. This is a favorite tactic of negotiators who use the "Soviet" style of bargaining. An outrageous offer is not a legitimate one.

Risk taking assessment — The basic rule of negotiating is not to take a risk unless you are completely aware of its implications and only if you have balanced the risk against what you gain. If you risk something, make sure you get something of equal value in return.

Commitment of parties — In order to survive and prosper, suppliers and customers must utilize a strategic negotiating plan in which both parties are committed to the principles of a win/win partnership. When there are rewards for both sides, each party is motivated to be a partner committed to cost reduction.

High ethics and morals — Only the highest ethics and morals are acceptable in business dealings. The best strategy is to steer clear of anybody or any company who even gives off a hint of impropriety.

Planning and expertise on topic — Determine your negotiating method and objectives. Negotiation today places a greater demand on a buyer's professionalism and understanding of the supplier base. The buyer must be part of a team which plans a strategy for purchasing quality items, delivered on time and at the lowest cost. This means that the buyer must be an expert negotiator who recognizes the most time should be spent on planning the negotiation.

Knowledge and proper attitude — The proper attitude is one of trust and cooperation. As successful companies, we need to develop a strategic plan to build products to customer satisfaction. We must keep negotiating as we design, purchase, build and sell. Negotiation is a strategic tool which will keep us continuously improving.

Power can also be attained through the use of body language. The flinch device is a visual reaction any time a proposal is made to you. For example, a friend of mine who does speaking engagements for $3,000 was negotiating with a company training director. The director told my friend that he might be interested, but that he couldn't pay more than $3,000.

My friend was about to say, "That's what I charge." Instead, he thought for a second and decided to try flinching.

"Three thousand?" he said. "I couldn't do it for that."

Right away, the training director came back with an "absolute maximum of $5,000." In ten seconds, my friend increased his profit by flinching.

POSITION

You can also increase your power through your position at the bargaining table. There have been many articles written about power seats and position in a room. We always like to be at position #8 in the illustrations on the next page, since this allows us to survey the whole room.

The seats of no power (#1, #3, #5, #7) command little respect in a discussion. At times, you may want to place your number two person in the power seat.

For example, in the illustrations on the next page, which number designates the power seat in an American negotiation session? Which number designates the power seat for a Japanese negotiating session? You can find the answers at the end of this chapter.

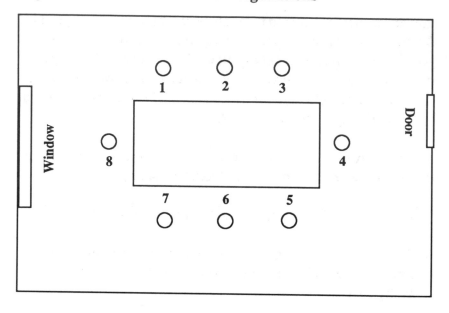

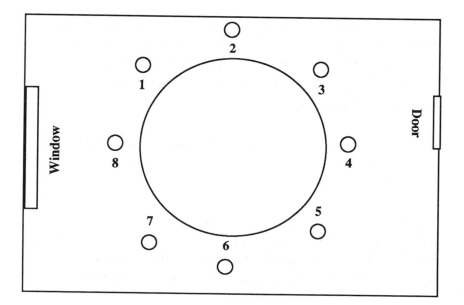

ESTABLISHING MIN/MAX LEVELS

Power in negotiation is also the result of having completed the planning process prior to the session. We suggest using a chart like the one shown here:

Task/Facts	Must Have	Min	Max	Reason

In the first column, list the tasks which you will be required to complete for each of the key elements that you need to accomplish. Put a check mark in the "Must Have" column if you cannot afford to compromise on a particular element. In the Min/Max columns, determine the limits of the range which your company will find acceptable. In the last column, put in post-negotiation session results to be used as material for future training exercises.

HOW TO DRESS FOR NEGOTIATIONS

When people are preparing for a negotiation session, it is extremely important to look respectable and to dress in a professional manner. Remember that your mission is to seek something for yourself or for your company. Clothes should be simple, neat, cleaned and pressed and non-revealing. For men, they should dress confidently and conventionally. Depending on the circumstances, you can wear either slacks and a sports coat or a dark suit. According to some experts, yellow or red ties denote power. For women, the same holds true as far as wearing clothes that express confidence, but which are conventional. Whether a man or a woman, you should not dress to stand out.

TIMING

Most people believe that negotiating is an event with a definite start and a definite conclusion. Negotiators walk into a meeting room, sit down at a table at 9 a.m. and hammer out a deal by 5 p.m. If you view negotiating in this manner, chances are that you will never negotiate the best deal. Buyers must look at negotiation as a process which begins far in advance of the actual negotiating session. Planning the negotiation process eliminates the pressure of making a quick deal where you don't get the lowest total cost. Planning also eliminates the type of negotiations where all the dealing is done at the eleventh hour, or just before a deadline.

DEADLINES

Power shifts quickly to the party which knows the other side's true deadline. All too often, a negotiator will give away more than necessary because he feels as though his back is up against a wall.

An example that comes to mind occurred on a trip to negotiate for power supply boards with a supplier in Korea. Upon arriving at the airport in Seoul, the seller's driver asked us what time our departing flight was scheduled to leave. At the time, we thought he wanted to coordinate getting the car with our departure. How wrong and naive we were! The driver had been instructed to find out our itinerary which he would then report to the supplier's sales group.

As the two-day visit progressed, we got bogged down on some issues which they suggested that we pass over until the end of negotiations. As the deadline for our departure neared, the pressure to make a deal or stay in Korea loomed larger and larger. To their surprise, we suggested a recess until the next day. They were even more surprised the next day when we appeared with our bags ready to go. The element of surprise and quick thinking are advantages. We didn't have the slightest idea if we could get a hotel or book a flight for the next day, but neither did they.

While negotiating, remember that no deadline is carved in stone. All deadlines are derived through some process of negotiation. That means they can be renegotiated. Proper timing insures that a buyer never appears too anxious to get her hands on a particular item at a particular time. Don't ever let a supplier know or believe that you have a deadline. Create the impression that similar items are readily available at comparable or better terms from different sources. You will gain the upper hand in negotiation if you do this.

LEAD-TIME

Too often, the buyer is put in the position of negotiating for a purchased part or service whose delivery date is not within the supplier's lead-time. This puts the buyer at a psychological disadvantage. Most companies do not track "the percentage of requests for purchase that violate supplier lead-time." We worked with one client and in eleven months, they went from 97 percent to 21 percent for requests of purchases that did not honor supplier lead-time. In addition, they reduced the average lead-time by 10 percent. This created a "can negotiate" atmosphere where one of harried firefighting had existed. If you have responsibility for the purchasing function, then you need to track and monitor requests that do not honor supplier lead-time. Work with related functions to monitor suppliers not honoring supplier lead-time on an on-going basis.

TIMING OF YOUR NEGOTIATIONS

1. **Be patient and calm as a deadline approaches.**

2. **Never reveal your true deadline.**

3. **Determine whether the other party's deadline is negotiable.**

4. **Look for creative win/win solutions as each deadline approaches.**

STRENGTHS AND WEAKNESSES

"Don't fight a battle, if you don't gain anything by winning."
— General George S. Patton, Jr.

Power and authority are perceived strengths. If you act as though you are in command, then your opponent will believe you are in command. In negotiations, if you believe you are the expert, then you are the expert. Always be positive about yourself, your bargaining position and the company you represent.

One of us, Paul Hine, has read the book, ***The Little Engine that Could***, over a hundred times and it is the gift he most often gives to young children. The little engine made it over the mountain because he believed he could. To psyche myself up prior to a negotiation, I repeat "I think I can" to myself. Positive imaging works. As we quoted Henry Ford earlier: "Those who think they can, and those who think they cannot, will prove themselves right in the end."

Never let your opponent know that you or the company are having trouble with this item or service. Conceding that your company is not top-rate tears your bargaining position to shreds. Be assertive and present yourself well. This includes personal appearance and demeanor. Don't be sloppy and don't appear disinterested.

Donald Trump, in his well-publicized troubles, could not hide his position. Consequently, when the negotiations to bail out Donald Trump's tumbling empire were underway, it was very difficult to get the many involved banks to agree on a course of action. The banks were being asked to defer interest and principal payments for up to five years, but they were able to get valuable collateral in return. Both the banks and Trump were able to fashion a win/win deal which turned a weakness into a strength.

INFORMATION

John Kennedy's rule in the White House was that "if there is more than one person (yourself) in a room, consider anything said to be on the record and a probable headline in the morning." You have to provide information to receive information in a win/win relationship. Don't wait until the last minute to get information about the other party. At that point, there is too much pressure and too little time. Both sides will try to conceal information, but you can trade the necessary information by doing the following:

- **Start early.**

- **Disarm the other party by being casual and by not intimidating them.**

- **Get information from everyone who is associated with the other party — secretaries, past customers, engineers.**

- **Look for the company's track record.**

- **Ask their competitors.**

Be careful when you share new information that you do it gradually and often in order to get the other side used to the new conditions. For example, if you have $1,000 to spend, don't open at $700 and then jump to $950. This gives the impression that you have more than $1,000. A better strategy is to start at $700 and then move to $750, then $825, then $875, and so on. The impression here is that it is more difficult to get you to move up, the closer you get to your spending limit. In other words, don't give the other party the wrong cues.

One of us, Pete Grieco, recently purchased a new motor yacht in which the negotiations took four months. When I went into negotiations, I knew that the timing was excellent from the buyer's perspective. Even though I didn't prequalify for the total purchase price from the seller, I figured that I could open up negotiations again if I went to the bank and got close to their bottom number.

After three months of going back and forth on the cost of the boat, I discovered that the model year had changed in August. Now, I told the sellers that I wanted a 1990 model instead of the 1989 model available at the factory. Of course, I didn't really care if my boat was built on August 31, 1989 or September 1, 1989. My objective was to keep the cost down because I planned on keeping the boat for a good number of years.

After not being able to get the financing I wanted, I simply told the sellers that I could not afford the yacht. The dealer then informed me that he might be able lower the price if I could come up with more cash. I told them I could and that I wanted them to show me the new price. It was substantially lower than our previous agreement.

I didn't have any more cash to spare, so I told the dealer that I would talk to the bank about a second position to come up with more money. Another month passed in which I was always in contact with the dealer (now my good friend). In November, I told him that the bank didn't have any way to take a second position, so we needed to relook the deal.

By this time, the manufacturer is ready to throw in a rebate on the 1989 boat. To make a long process short, we bought the boat in January at a 27 percent reduction from the original contract price.

BARRIERS

The time will come when your negotiations meet problems and barriers which seem impossible to overcome. At this point, you should never resort to embarrassing opponents. Don't put them in an awkward position in the eyes of their peers or superiors. Embarrassing only serves to make people angry and uncooperative. As we have said before, if you can't work with the other negotiator, let somebody else take your place at the table. Don't be afraid to tell the opposing negotiator that things aren't working and that you're going to make a switch so as to help the process move along.

Breaking down barriers is a difficult process which requires patience. For example, when selling his home in Connecticut, Pete Grieco was approached by a buyer who made a ridiculously low offer. The buyer tried the "Soviet" tactic of "take it or leave it." Pete left it. He kept coming back every few days. Finally, he didn't come back anymore and my agent said that the chance of a deal was dead because I didn't accept the man's final offer.

In order to break this barrier, I told the agent to inform my agent that a new offer would be on the table at 5 p.m. from a third party and that I would not negotiate with two people. This was at 3 p.m., so the buyer had two hours to reconsider my last offer. You guessed it — I sold the house.

"SOVIET" STYLE NEGOTIATION

Before Mikhail Gorbachev, a negotiating opponent who always returned to a stonewall position, unwilling to budge, was known as a "Soviet" style negotiator. It is a win/lose style of negotiation.

Here are some other ways to recognize this style:

- Negotiators start with ridiculous offers.
- They have little or no authority to make concessions.
- They use emotional tactics (Remember Khrushchev pounding the table with his shoe?)
- They view concessions as signs of weakness.
- They act as if they have all the time in the world.
- They make you react emotionally.
- They break the rules without concern.
- Their desires know no limits.
- Winning is everything.

"Soviet" negotiators always start with an extreme opening position. For example, if a product is worth $10,000 on the market, these negotiators will ask for $15,000. When you reply that this is unacceptable, they will flare up and say, "This is my final offer. Take it or leave it. I won't go any lower." If you make a concession and come up to $11,000, they will either not budge or come down to $14,900. Recognize this negotiator? How can you deal with this style?

We often make the mistake of thinking the Soviets are strong, loud and demanding. Paul's daughter Lisa taught him that Soviets can also be soft, sweet and crying. When Lisa was five years old, Paul discovered her practicing how to fall flat on the floor so that she could begin crying. The "Nikitas" of the world may be easier to spot, but like his daughter they learn very early to practice.

When given a fine display of an emotional tactic, compliment the "Soviet" by asking to see the performance again. Never, however, get pulled into an emotional war with a "Soviet" because they will win.

The most effective method for fighting this style of negotiating is to recognize the tactics and then let the other side know that *you know* what is going on. Tell the seller that he has to do his homework and quote you a reasonable number. You have to be willing to walk out and not look back. Don't respond to ridiculous offers and measly concessions as though they were realistic. Let the seller know that you want a fair price and true value for this negotiation.

When a negotiator of this type confronts you with a time limit on his offer, this is how to respond. He says, "You have to tell me if we're going to sign this contract by Monday or else the deal is off." Our recommendation is to call his bluff. It's an arbitrary deadline. Don't phone until Wednesday. Nine times out of ten he will call you back to start talking again.

Likewise, if the seller tells you that he has another offer for the item, tell him to go ahead and sell. Call his bluff. Usually, he will still negotiate and you will have shifted bargaining strength to your side. You've taken him away from his win/lose position. But remember what Mark Hatfield said, "Never get into a spraying match with a skunk."

A friend of ours was buying a home in California and asked for some help. On a trip out there, we spent time looking at the area. We noticed that there were several homes for sale on the street where his potential new home was located. Our strategy, which was in response to "Soviet" style negotiating on the other side, was to make two offers at the same time. One offer had his address on it; the other had the address of his neighbor across the street who was also selling. We told him to pick one. If he had said "no" at that point, we would have made another offer, but it wasn't necessary. This approach gave the owner of our first choice the option of letting us buy his neighbor's property. Put yourself in his place. Would you want to sell your house or your neighbor's?

NEGOTIATING IN JAPAN

Here's an example of how to handle certain negotiations in Japan. When I worked for Apple, we went on a trip to Japan to negotiate the RAM required for Apple's laser printer. Our purchasing team consisted of people from purchasing, operations, engineering and Steve Jobs. The component manufacturer arranged to meet us at Narita airport and bring us to a formal dinner party in our honor. The agenda for the next day and a half was as follows:

Introduction/Dinner	7 p.m. to whenever
Pick-up at hotel next morning	7 a.m.
Arrival at plant	8:30 a.m.
Presentation of opening positions	9:00 a.m. - 11 a.m.
Plant visit	11 a.m. - noon
Lunch	Noon - 1 p.m.
Engineering/tech discussions	1 p.m. - 3 p.m.
Logistics	3 p.m. - 4 p.m.
Concluding negotiations	4 p.m. - 5 p.m.

Depart to hotel	5 p.m.
Dinner (Tokyo)	7 p.m. to whenever

As you can see, the idea was to keep us busy and wear us down after our long trip. Japanese business dinners, for example, are long affairs which usually conclude with a nightcap at a sing-along establishment. Steve Jobs had little patience with this process. He treated the negotiations as an event. In fact, on several occasions, he upset our host by trying to talk exclusively about price. At one point, after informing our host that he could get a better deal from another OEM supplier, negotiations were abruptly halted. Since we had opened with a radical approach, we now turned the process into a hostile encounter. What should have taken one or two days ended up taking almost two weeks. We would have been better off, I believe, to heed the old saying which says, "When in Rome, do as the Romans do."

The Japanese use the following techniques when they negotiate:

- Patience.
- Pride.
- Technology, R & D strength.
- Teamwork.
- Quality.
- Win/win.
- Trust.

In the negotiations described above, all we did was alienate our supplier and violate his trust. Their team of negotiators lost face and a win/win really turned out to be a win/lose. The lesson is that we must make sure that the style we present is the true style and message that we want to deliver. If it is, then we will avoid problems at the negotiating table.

DEADLOCKS

A deadlock occurs when a material change of position is no longer possible. A deadlock, unlike a deadline which says this is the end of the negotiating process, amounts to both parties reaching unacceptable positions. If the process ever does come to a stop, we recommend that each side summarize its position. We even suggest writing each side's summary on a board.

Another way to break a deadlock is to introduce new blood, information or data. What is required is the necessity of establishing a common base for movement.

Mike Gozzo, my good friend and Executive Vice President of Pro-Tech, recently wanted to buy a Porsche. He visited the dealer each week for three months. He test drove numerous cars and said that he wanted one. However, he told the dealer, your price is out of line. Nobody pays the sticker price for a car. The salesperson said that the dealership's policy was to sell at sticker price. Mike's response was that the salesperson should call him when the dealership has changed its policy. Seven months have gone by and Mike is still driving his old car. Maybe next year, he told the salesperson. This is a deadlock: neither party wants to move.

PREPARING FOR THE GAME OF NEGOTIATION

"Never play cat and mouse, if you are the mouse."
— **Paul Dickson**

Professionals know the secret of preparation as a major tactic. Where do you find the golf pro before the match? At the practice tee. Where do you find the duffer? At the nineteenth hole. It takes time to prepare for a negotiation. Managers in this country don't devote enough time to preparation, strategy and research. When negotiating for a supply deal worth millions of dollars, the benefit or preparation is obvious. Saving two percent on $20,000,000 is a significant amount of money.

Think of negotiation as an ongoing process, not a one-time event. All athletes know that years of training result in the gold medal. Make sure that you understand what you want and find out what the supplier wants. Remember that a professional approach will pay off. This includes coaching anyone who will be involved with the negotiations, whether they are doing research or exchanging information. Preparing for negotiation is like preparing for a big game. Even though only one person may actually negotiate, he or she must have a team to provide support in order to obtain the best possible results. Teamwork is effective. Its results are clear.

The following story shows why. Mary L. Aaron, a purchasing specialist at International Totalizator Systems, Inc., relates that in her internal negotiations she found out both Engineering and Marketing had come up with a price of $224 for a new PGA ceramic ASIC package. After looking at two Japanese ceramic PGA manufacturers as possible suppliers of this new product, Supplier "K" was chosen as the preferred source by Engineering because of the company's strong technical expertise in producing complex, state-of-the-art PGAs.

Supplier "K's" initial quote, however, was $365, based on a potential forecast of 1,000 packages for the first year. She informed them that the bid was unacceptable and that they needed to lower the cost substantially in order to be competitive. She waited for two weeks while the "K" American sales office negotiated with their Japanese corporate sales office. The supplier then informed her that they couldn't drop the price as low as she wanted because of the complexity of the parts. They also told her that another key factor was the unpredictable forecast for this new product. After that, they requoted her at $310.

Mary then proceeded to negotiate again with the American office to lower the cost further. After a week and a half, the response from Japan was $275 and "That was final!" She told the American office that the price was still not acceptable and that it could seriously impede a major product as well as future ASIC packages of similar design. Knowing that the manager of the Japanese sales office was in America, Mary invited him to her facility for the final round of negotiations.

Part of the strategy, she says, was to meet on her turf in her company's smallest conference room. The room was directly outside of a busy lobby where there was standing room only. She made sure that her Japanese visitor was aware of the competitors in that lobby as he signed in. When Mary and her Japanese counterpart finally met, she followed traditional Japanese protocol, bowing and presenting him with her business card. When they entered the small conference room, she sat at the head of the small oval table with her engineering manager (whom she had discussed strategy with earlier) to her right. The "K" people, five in all, filled the remaining places at the table.

The discussion began with the representative from "K's" American sales office, explaining their need to keep the pricing as is. The

Japanese visitor said nothing, took some notes and nodded his head occasionally. After a brief reiteration by our engineering manager of the creativity, technical impact and long-term dynamics of this new package, she finally threw out her trump card. She told the assembled group that the bottom line was the cost. If she could not get the cost established by marketing for this PGA, the entire project would be canceled including any future R&D efforts for such a product. She told them that this was simply a make or break deal for her company.

After the meeting, they shook hands and parted. She waited one week for what was promised to be the final "final" offer (now that the Japanese visitor had been "properly informed about the nature of the situation"). At the end of the week, she received a FAX, followed by an excited phone call from "K's" American representative, saying that the final offer was $213. Eventually, she went on to order 50,000 units which she renegotiated for $152 each.

LOCATION CONSIDERATIONS

The easiest way to use your full team is to negotiate first on your own site or at your own factory. Then, if a question comes up that you can't handle, you can get on the phone and call up the person who does know the answer. It's even possible for that specialist to come in for five minutes or so to help you handle that particular trouble spot. At the supplier's site (the last choice), this is almost impossible. If you want your team with you, it will cost your company transportation and lodging. And, the longer the negotiation takes, the more money your company has to spend to keep you all there. You can be sure that your opponent will be aware of that situation. A good negotiator will have already negotiated internally so that the team can walk into negotiation with the opponent knowing exactly what the people back at the plant need. They also know what their min/max levels are.

The second choice for a negotiation session is a neutral site. Since both parties will need to travel, there is a better chance of reaching a win/win conclusion.

TEAMWORK

If you think your team can win a negotiation, then you can win. Faith and trust are necessary for winning. The company which forms a negotiation team will have more successes than the company which sends buyers out to forge for themselves. Yes, the team approach takes more time and effort, but that is required in order to lower the total cost.

HAVE FUN

Donald Trump says that negotiating should be fun because life is so fragile. We agree. Negotiations should be fun in order to gain total company involvement. Having fun requires a lot of energy and hard work, but it pays off. With success comes rewards and the excitement from seeing your hard work produce satisfying results. What you gain, a new level of experience, may be the most rewarding result of a successful negotiation.

When the process of negotiation is fun to be involved in, that also makes it easier to "clone for success." Other divisions, other salespeople will see how happy your team is about what you are doing. They will want to join in and find out the secrets of your success. In the long run, it pays to make what you are doing as enjoyable as possible.

Answers to questions on Page 146:
          American — #8
          Japanese — #2 or #6

CHAPTER SEVEN

"The best things in life are free, with or without negotiation."
— Mary Aaron

Chapter Seven

SAVING MONEY

At one time or another, we are all faced with the need to reduce costs. When this happens, don't immediately get on the phone and demand a percentage reduction. We must involve the other party and provide a sound explanation of why our costs need to be reduced. The other party isn't going to take its profit margin and give it to you just because you asked. Reducing costs leaves you with three choices:

1. Negotiate with current supplier.

2. Search for alternate source.

3. Work with the current party to reduce costs.

LOOKING FOR A NEW SOURCE
OR AN ALTERNATIVE SOLUTION

Sometimes looking for a new source or an alternative solution is the best avenue to pursue in order to get the required savings.

There is, however, a certain amount of risk in changing suppliers. Analyze the situation you are in and then objectively evaluate how many of the problems are of your own making. The new source may be less able to deal with your problems than your current source. As part of your planning when changing sources, put together a checklist for the transition. One of the items on your checklist should be whether your company will need to build up inventory in the event that the new source does not perform on schedule.

When looking for a new source, you may be able to find a supplier with lower overhead rates, a more automated facility, a more efficient operation or more available inventory. For example, if you are purchasing a new car and cannot get the best deal from the dealer, it is time to search out new sources. Don't let your emotions sway you from this decision. If you keep saying "All I want is *this* car," the seller will have the upper hand. As we discussed earlier, shopping around without a plan will result in higher costs for the buyer in the end. The planning process is of significant value.

A good planning process rests on a sound philosophy: establish a target for the sellers which will allow them to meet your requirements. Part of your planning also has to include identifying and getting the approval and input of the other functions within your company who need to approve the changing of sources. When the customer (you) is flexible about color, style, model and even the manufacturer, that is when the best possible deal can be struck. This situation will not occur with a high pressure sales force breathing down your neck, telling you that you have to buy today (the one-day special price). This approach makes you buy on emotions, not facts, and causes you to deviate from the negotiation plan. Such a course of action is not conducive to the kind of win/ win relationship which is desirable in the long run for the continuous satisfaction of both parties.

HOW *NOT* TO SWITCH SOURCES

Many companies get confused when they see a lower price quoted. They think that the lower price automatically translates into a cost reduction. Two years ago, one of our clients was shocked when they were informed by a customer that it would no longer be ordering product from our client. This buyer's orders amounted to over $950,000 per year. What was even more surprising was that three months prior to the notification of no more orders, our client had just completed a lengthy process which resulted in Part Certification status for the last of eight parts which were supplied to the customer.

Although the customer's Quality Assurance function was behind the supplier certification program, the customer's Purchasing function decided to seek an annualized quote from a competitor of our client. When the quote came in at $55,000 less, the customer elected to stop doing any more business with a fully certified partner. It was a very costly decision for them. They found out the hard way what the difference is between price and cost.

The new supplier, as a result of quality and delivery problems, caused our client's former customer to shut down its production line seven times. In addition, production line efficiency was reduced by 14 percent when it was running. All of this, of course, resulted in lost sales due to the inability to make shipments.

The Purchasing manager at our client's former customer was put in the awkward position of calling our client and asking them if they would take their business back. Our client was willing to do this, but only if the customer would agree to a five-year contract at an increase in price. Needless to say, under the circumstance, the customer was very willing to accept.

WORKING WITH YOUR CURRENT SOURCE

Here is where a little creative negotiating comes into play with your partner. A certain percentage of total cost reduction must be the focal point of our efforts. The attitude to take with suppliers is a "let's sit down together and research the problem" approach. Both parties will need to evaluate the product itself and its production process through value analysis and by working together in order to cut costs. Suppliers should be motivated and rewarded for the cost-saving ideas they develop. If the suppliers are offered a percentage of cost-savings resulting from accepted ideas, then they will be motivated and a true win/win cost reduction effort will be in place.

A Value Engineering approach to reduce the cost of a product is worthwhile and needs to be established as a continuous process, not as just a one-time occurrence. Value Engineering focuses on the function of the product and seeks to eliminate anything that does not serve a function, but does add to the cost. Value Engineering can be used on products and on services. It is a technique used to identify unnecessary costs, remove any obstacles which are keeping them there, and to create value-oriented alternatives from which to choose. It aims to reduce the hidden costs in almost all products by analyzing the areas depicted in the table on the following page.

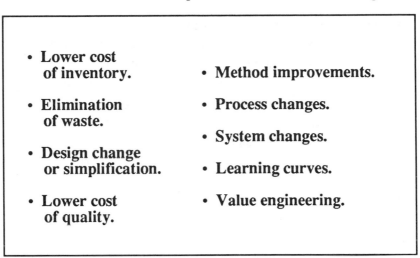

- **Lower cost of inventory.**

- **Elimination of waste.**

- **Design change or simplification.**

- **Lower cost of quality.**

- **Method improvements.**

- **Process changes.**

- **System changes.**

- **Learning curves.**

- **Value engineering.**

Some of the most productive and dramatic cost savings will be achieved through Value Engineering when we ask the question, "What are we doing and why are we doing it?" as many times as necessary in order to achieve the desired cost objectives.

VALUE ENGINEERING EDUCATION

During a recent negotiation session in Japan, we found that the supplier's costs far exceeded our Design to Cost (DTC) goals and objectives. After spending three days on terms, conditions and cost, we appeared to be at a dead end. During a caucus, our team recapped our position and that of our supplier. Based on our planning process for this session, we all agreed that our cost objectives and the supplier's profit level were fair.

We then decided to recess the negotiations so both parties could study the other's position. We asked the supplier to restate its position and to write a response to ours, and we would do the same. Before we could adjourn, the supplier immediately jumped up and went to the flip chart where he began to outline their position. During the presentation, we discovered that many of the Design for Producibility standards we wanted were not included in their cost breakdowns. Although the supplier was, in our opinion, a World Class supplier of disk drives, the company lacked some of the fundamental assembly rules needed to reduce costs.

Our Engineering Manager quickly took the opportunity to provide a quick overview on the merits of tooling, assembly rules and the elimination of cost at various operations. The net result was a 23 percent cost decrease, eight less components to purchase and eight less additional suppliers. We were also able to eliminate future component assembly in our own plant.

CHANGING SPECIFICATIONS

When Paul Hine was Director of Materials for an emergency lighting company, he discovered that the light sockets used in their indoor EXIT signs were giving them trouble. At the same time, he was coming under extreme pressure to keep the cost of the sign's components down as they were under attack in the marketplace for pricing. Although their socket supplier produced high quality parts at a very favorable price, he had delivery problems which were due to production problems with the socket. Paul then decided to visit the supplier with his Design Engineering Manager to help them resolve the problem.

After reviewing their materials and manufacturing cycle, they met with key people at their plant to give them their findings and recommendations for improvement. They reached agreement on all the points, but the supplier's president and owner told them that, although he could keep the pricing stable, he still could do no better than 80 to 85 percent on-time delivery performance. He based this figure on the current six-week lead-time.

Paul told him that they needed to work together to reduce the lead-time, increase the on-time delivery performance and do something about pricing since our average sales price on a unit was dropping. To their surprise, the owner countered with another proposal.

"Would you be satisfied with a 33 percent reduction in lead-time, my personal guarantee of 100 percent on-time delivery and an 11 percent drop in price?"

He went on to inform Paul that the white socket his company was specifying was the problem, but if they could use a black socket, then he could guarantee the previously stated promises. He could do this because the white resin used in the manufacturing of white sockets was difficult to purchase and caused processing problems.

He gave Paul samples of the black sockets so his company could test them. Sure enough, they worked fine and were not visible from outside the sign. A difficult problem was solved with a very simple change. The actual reduction in lead-time was 50 percent, instead of 33, with 100 percent on-time delivery. This enabled his company to reduce inventory substantially with an 11 percent price reduction as a bonus.

SUPPLIER TECHNIQUES

It is the responsibility of both parties to look closely at all processes and systems for cost reduction opportunities. These areas are overlooked elements that have not been examined in the past.

Other issues that must be addressed:

- Can some part of the deal be changed?

- Is the supplier using state-of-the-art techniques?

- Is it feasible to rent or lease space to the supplier so that he can produce internally as required?

- Determine the method and alternatives for transportation.

- Separate all costs to the lowest element.

- If you're buying through a distributor, can you go back to the Original Equipment Manufacturer (OEM)?

- Can you combine your purchases with other people or divisions to achieve greater discounts through volume?

- Do you understand the supplier's process?

- Review packaging specifications and employ reusable containers to reduce costs.

SPC (Statistical Process Control) AND COST REDUCTION

In a recent negotiation class, one of our delegates asked a question which we'd like to share with you.

> Dr. Lee Ann Zunich, purchasing manager for Morton International Specialty Chemicals Group, was having problems reducing the cost of a container for liquids. All her efforts ended with no satisfactory solutions. As we started to probe her issue in the class, we learned that she received a high percent of defective bottles from her supplier. She called these bottles "leakers" because the cap would not fit properly and the liquid leaked out.
>
> Our suggestion was to work with the supplier to improve the quality of the components. We decided first to provide the supplier with training in Statistical Process Control (SPC). Our reasoning was that once they got their process under control, we could talk about cost reduction.
>
> In a recent discussion with her, she told us that she had no problems with the supplier after taking our suggestions. As a matter of fact, she was so pleased that she has told this story to numerous people.
>
> In today's business environment, we need to use a different approach in solving cost reduction problems. Only a few years ago, the solution above would have made management very angry. "Why are we training a source? It's their responsibility." With a win/win approach, however, each party must help the other so that both parties can win.

TRAFFIC ANALYSIS

When Paul created the function of a traffic analyst at an established, multinational firm in New England, the trees were full of low-hanging fruit. New items had been added to one of the plant's product lines, but the bills of lading had not been updated to include these new products. Researching one of the new products, he discovered that the common carrier had been charging the highest applicable rate, Class 150, since the company had not assigned a specific classification to the product.

By reading through the motor freight classification guide and by working with salesmen from the common carrier, Paul came up with a specific classification. This resulted in the product being a Class 60 item which meant a 60 percent reduction in the freight rate applied to each shipment. Within one month, he had properly classified all items shipped from each plant. The new classifications were preprinted on their bills of lading. The first year goal was for the traffic analyst to reduce overall freight expenditures by five percent. The actual reduction for the first year was 11 percent. This is yet another form of negotiations which serves to drive down costs.

BRAINSTORMING COST REDUCTIONS

Brainstorming, as stated in an earlier chapter, is a traditional technique used to solve business problems. We believe the use of this approach with each of your suppliers will result in both lower cost and higher quality. Cost reduction through brainstorming is a dynamic process, but it will only achieve the desired results when your source is totally involved.

Each negotiating team involved in cost reduction should go through the following steps with their source:

- **Determine the symptoms. (Why costs are high.)**
- **Identify possible causes. (Areas of waste.)**
- **Verify root causes of problem. (Why high costs exist.)**
- **Find ways to eliminate problem. (Lower total cost.)**
- **Select the way with the lowest cost. (Win/win.)**

Tom Peters, at a recent talk, told the assembled businesspeople that if companies did not know how to do fishbone diagrams soon, they would be educationally deficient. Fishbones are tremendous brainstorming tools when used properly. In a partnership, all parties should list each possible cause by category. Prior to posting the list of all the causes, they should be categorized.

As the cause and effect (fishbone) diagram on the next page shows, the intent is to identify a problem (high cost) and its possible causes and then to note which causes are being worked on and which are complete. Each diagram is a visual reminder of progress as well as what specific cause can be attributed to higher costs.

SHARING DATA

Ethically, a buyer should not reveal prices quoted by competing suppliers. But there are numerous ways of keeping costs in line without violating this rule. One such way is a "meet competition" clause. A buyer negotiates a clause in which all suppliers must meet the lowest cost of the other suppliers. When this is done "up-front," it becomes part of the agreement with each supplier.

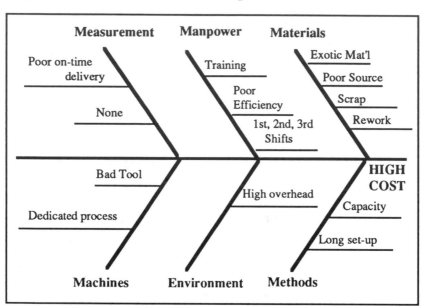

Cause Enumeration Fishbone

The "meet competition" clause can be a very useful tool for the buyer. Let's say one supplier is charging $1.05, a second is charging $1.00 and the third is charging $0.90. The buyer shows suppliers A and B that supplier C is charging $0.90. At the same time, the buyer works with supplier C through value analysis to continue reducing the cost.

Your purchasing professionals are probably asking how the example above is win/win. The answer lies in the answer to the question of whether a glass is half full or half empty. When you negotiate a "meet competition" clause up-front, each source enters the agreement with eyes open. We agree that this approach would be win/lose if a partnership had already been established. If supplier C continued to work with you under this agreement to lower costs, they would not get the full reward for being the low cost producer. That reward should be all of your business. Supplier C may soon start to feel that you are using them to beat the other suppliers down in price.

Another negative quality of this negotiating method is that it assumes that the supplier with the lowest price is the best one. Supplier A, B and C may not be equal when it comes to quality, total cost, design engineering support, on-time delivery, etc. It would be better to choose the best supplier for the application and then work with that supplier to help them reduce costs. Do not overlook the fact that the goal of both suppliers and customers is to lower total cost in order for each side to make a profit. As a standard rule, we believe that the supplier's profit percentage should continue to improve as yours does.

THE THREE-BID PROCESS

The problem with the three-bid process is that it was developed to satisfy accountants who thought that the best supplier was the one with the lowest price and as a method to eliminate corruption. We believe that a good buyer should be able to pick the best supplier without the three-bid process. Choosing the lowest price supplier should be justified in writing. Our goal is to achieve the best cost and highest quality first. We must develop partners who:

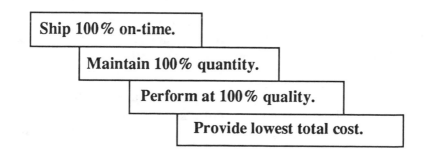

Ship 100% on-time.

Maintain 100% quantity.

Perform at 100% quality.

Provide lowest total cost.

Price is not, you will notice, a goal. In order for your company to reorient themselves to this modern approach, you will need to involve your financial group in the negotiation process in order to help you discover what the lowest cost possible can be. Developing a Total Cost model is not easy, but if your company is committed to the lowest total cost concept, there needs to be a way to calculate it, not just to give it lip service. Finance should participate in the development of a Total Cost model and should approve of its use.

TARGET PRICING

The method of target pricing can also be used in the win/win approach. When Peter Grieco worked for Apple's Macintosh factory, he helped establish target pricing for all components and assemblies during the early stages of product development. The company's objective was to bring a product to market that was lower than Design to Cost (DTC) goals. Their approach was to select the best supplier for each commodity and then to ask the suppliers to work with them in early design stages to obtain the best cost.

This is called target pricing. This allows the supplier to design a product that can realistically meet established cost targets. This is somewhat the reverse of setting parameters in which you list features and specifications. Here you provide a cost as the parameter and let the supplier participate in the designing of a product to meet cost objectives and quality requirements.

It is becoming very common for Engineering, Quality and Purchasing to select a supplier together at the design concept stage and then to share Design to Cost parameters and other pertinent information with the supplier. In such an arrangement, the supplier works on the design with the knowledge that they are the chosen supplier for the part.

SUPPLIER CAPABILITY

Suppose you want to buy 100,000 rowboats and need to find a source. One strategy is to do some research and find out who manufactures rowboats and ask them to submit sealed bids. When you have selected the lowest bidder, you can then negotiate specifications and terms based on that price. The other strategy is to investigate the capability and quality of the best World Class rowboat manufacturers. Once you have selected the best supplier for the job, then negotiate with the most qualified source. This can only be accomplished by using a supplier survey as detailed in my book, **SUPPLIER CERTIFICATION:** *Achieving Excellence* (PT Publications, Inc., Palm Beach Gardens, FL).

WAVING THE BIG STICK

We do not recommend this approach with a partner, but there are times when a buyer must be hard-nosed, unwilling to negotiate or willing to walk away. The smart buyer knows that these tactics should only be used sparingly. These tactics result in a win/lose agreement. Remember, too, that there is a difference between suppliers and vendors. A vendor is somebody you infrequently purchase an item from—hot dogs, peanuts or beer at a baseball game. A supplier is a partner. Don't use heavy-handed tactics with partners.

One day as Paul Hine sat at his desk at a company where he was the Director of Materials, the President/Owner and Vice President of Marketing for one of his suppliers walked into the office. They represented one of the company's largest suppliers and had a cozy relationship with the Engineering department. The owner proceeded to sit down and take a sheet of paper out of his briefcase.

"Here is your new price sheet which represents a 5% increase, effective in two weeks," he said.

Without a word, Paul took the paper from him and crumpled it into a ball which he threw into the wastebasket. The owner got angry and told him that he couldn't do that, whereupon the owner handed over another price sheet. Paul crumpled that sheet into a ball and threw it into the wastebasket.

"I'm enjoying the basketball practice," Paul informed the owner, "and I'm sure you will get tired of handing me price sheets long before I tire of throwing them in the basket. If you want to discuss pricing in the future, please give me notice of that prior to your visit. For now, there is no price increase."

This bought Paul some time and resulted in no change in price. Each of those baskets was worth about $30,000 to his company. His actions also established the Materials function as one which would not be dictated to. On the negative side, however, he found out that the owner was taken aback by his approach to the price increase. So, although heavy-handed tactics can be effective, they often leave wounds.

REWARDING SUPPLIERS

Suppliers should also be rewarded. An effective cost reduction program should result in better margins for the supplier as well as the purchaser. The easiest way to reward a supplier is to pay him as soon as possible. Another way to reward the supplier is to insure that their profit picture and percentage continue to improve. This means sharing part of the cost savings.

We deal with thousands of purchasing professionals at our public seminars and we always ask them how many of their companies pay on-time. We find that less than half do. So, if your company does pay on-time, this gives you leverage, but you must make sure your supplier knows that you pay on time during the negotiations. Otherwise, there may be a tacking on of an extra percentage based upon anticipated late payment.

LIFE OF THE PRODUCT

When a supplier shares in the research and development of a product, they will want to recoup any outlays. If a supplier believes the buyer is going to deal with him for only a short period of time, then it may not be worth putting money into the product.

Both supplier and buyer benefit, however, when a long-term relationship exists. In asking a supplier to assist in the design of a particular component, the buyer should commit to a long-term agreement. In Japan, under these circumstances, the buyer promises to buy from that supplier for the life of the product. This is what every supplier wants to hear. To keep the item, the supplier must perform to the agreement.

In a long-term relationship, you want to make sure that the supplier's key people are familiar with the insides of your operation. They should thoroughly understand how the product they supply will be used and assembled. With this knowledge, your supplier will be able to give you ideas about how to reduce costs, improve assembly operations and make the product more reliable.

SOURCE OF SUPPLY

Visiting your source of supply benefits your cost-reduction efforts. By having first-hand knowledge of the site, you learn numerous facts about their operation and how it works. The more we know about the other party, the better off we are. When we teach a negotiation education and training program, we ask how many participants visit their suppliers more than once a year. The answer we normally get is that suppliers are only visited when there is trouble.

At the Apple Macintosh plant, we established a goal of visiting each supplier at least two times a year. We also requested our partners to visit us the same number of times. During these visits, we could conduct value analysis, review cost structures and data such as cost of quality and cost of inventory.

When you do visit a supplier, keep your purpose in mind. You should be there to help your supplier become a World Class Competitor. Many companies survey their suppliers as if they were conducting an inquisition. Rather than helping the suppliers, the companies start dictating what changes the supplier has to make. No one likes to be told what to do. Surveys should be done from a win/win perspective where both parties feel that the survey was a worthwhile endeavor that everybody learned from. Instead of using surveys to catch your supplier doing something wrong, use them to help your supplier get better and to strengthen your partnership.

If the steel industry had listened to what customers truly wanted, it wouldn't be in such bad shape today. It looked as though the industry was going to turn around, but large steel companies are in another bad slump. Meanwhile, small steel companies have catered to the customer. At the same time, large steel companies told customers how much to buy, when to buy and how much it would cost. The small mills realized that all customers wanted was fast delivery and excellent quality each and every time. It certainly seems like a window was missed again.

MAKE OR BUY

Frequently a company will find itself in a situation where it must decide whether to make or buy an item. To decide which course to take, a company should investigate the market rate for the purchase and delivery of that item. Then, it should calculate the cost of manufacturing or price/cost. If you need assistance in setting up and establishing a formula, get assistance from your finance group. Costs should include the following:

- Labor rate.
- Facility cost.
- Facility capacity to manufacture the item.
- Customer service.
- Overhead structure. (Compared to supply base structure.)
- Cost of quality.
- Cost of inventory.
- Freight/transportation.

Calculating internal costs can be complicated. The overhead of producing the product internally will appear lower or higher because much of the manufacturing process may not already be in place. It's important to consider that the supplier's initial overhead may be higher because he must develop the structure to begin production and delivery. Also, be aware that higher wages may not mean better labor. Wages are, in part, a function of where the plant is located. Be fair to the supplier when performing a "make or buy" analysis.

As a rule of thumb, a buyer should expect the external cost to be higher than internal costs. A supplier who can produce for 120 percent of the internal production costs is usually quoting an equitable price. This guideline is dependent upon the specific job being quoted. A supplier using automatic equipment, for example, will charge a higher rate to cover overhead costs.

When performing a "make or buy" analysis, the buyer should fully examine why the supplier is quoting that particular price. A higher price might be acceptable if the buyer's plant is running at capacity already. Consider that any additional workload may overburden production facilities. The bottom line is to find out which course of action will cost less, why it will cost less, and for how long will it cost less.

Most important of all, determine who is the highest quality producer today and who is most likely to continue to be the highest quality producer in the future. Cost reduction begins with a plan of what your maximum and minimum levels will be. Set these levels and go into negotiation with a clear idea of what you are willing to pay.

CHAPTER EIGHT

"I've won before, I've lost before
... winning is definitely better."
— Peter L. Grieco, Jr. and Paul G. Hine

INTERFACE REQUIREMENTS

INTERFACING

A company must have sound communication and interfacing between employees in all functions within the structure: engineering, quality, manufacturing, purchasing, sales and finance. A win/win style of negotiating requires all participants to understand and commit themselves to the goal and objectives of the mission and to why it is important. As we mentioned in the planning section, it is helpful to meet with all involved parties. The more information which is gathered throughout the company, the more successful the negotiations will be.

SUPPLIER INVOLVEMENT

We have found that the best way to obtain the lowest cost is to involve the sellers early in the process. When you are developing a new product, include the suppliers you will be using in the product concept meetings. In this way, the supplier can learn what you want early in the development process. At the same time, the supplier can inform you of any obstacles or impediments which may cause the component price not to meet the Design to Cost (DTC) goals.

For example, let's say that Computer Company XYZ is designing a new personal computer system. Company XYZ chooses its tooling and injection molding supplier before the components are designed. At the same time, Company XYZ is designing components with feedback from its suppliers who are normally the experts in the field. As a result, the supplier is keyed into the process from the start. They work with you to reduce cost and complications prior to placing a purchase order. Both sides benefit from this approach, the result being lower costs and components which are easier to manufacture and of consistent quality.

Ordinarily, a company designs a component and then targets a specific price for each item. These prices are then brought to the Purchasing department who must find a supplier with less expensive prices. This traditional method where Engineering completes the design and then throws it to Purchasing to find a supplier using the bidding process is expensive. In excess of 80 percent of a component's cost is locked in, once the drawing has been made. The supplier is often left with no alternative, but to quote the part as designed even if the design is expensive and difficult to produce reliably. This sorry state of affairs can be avoided by bringing the supplier into the process early. Make your cost objectives and target prices his cost-cutting goals.

In this win/win environment, both the supplier and buyer develop mutual trust which makes a long-term arrangement more likely. Suppliers, of course, find long-term agreements to be desirable. It assures them of consistent revenue. When a purchaser approaches a supplier and asks them to develop a product within certain specifications, the supplier requires some reassurance that the deal will pay off for the company over the long run. More specifically, if a supplier becomes part of your design team, they will want assurance that they will get the order. Many companies have damaged their reputation by working with one supplier during the design phase, then putting the part out to bid and selecting another supplier for production. This can happen if Purchasing and Engineering do not work together in a synergistic relationship when selecting a supplier.

ENGINEERING

Our message here is to use a buyer as the person to negotiate cost and the engineer to review methods, processes and technology. We have seen many companies where buyers are involved after the fact, when in fact they should have been the ones initiating the process and introducing the supplier to the Engineering group. When one of us, Pete, worked at Digital Equipment Corporation (DEC), they used to allow their engineers to buy products and components on a personal VISA or MasterCard. When the Purchasing group asked why this practice was allowed, we were told that Purchasing does not respond quickly enough to their urgent needs. When the engineers followed the rules, it took two weeks to process a piece of paper (the purchase order) and four to five days for the part to get out of Receiving. It only took two hours to get the part through the door and on the engineer's desk using the charge card method. The solution was to place a full-time buyer in the engineering department to support engineering activity. When we did this, the buyer became part of the engineering team. The result was a 25 percent reduction in purchasing costs compared to the previous year.

Design engineering normally figures prominently into the negotiation process. Think about the components used in your company today. Do they need to be as complex and expensive as they are? Can a less expensive item perform the exact same task? Do you even need the component at all?

The main goal and objective of an engineer is to get the job done right the first time. Engineers are not generally trained in the art of working with suppliers as purchasing agents are. The combination of an engineer and buyer, however, can create a powerful image which will correctly start off the negotiation and cost-cutting process with a third party. This is the most desirable arrangement from a negotiations perspective for this type of objective.

Here is a question you need to ask at your company:

**Are Engineering and Purchasing
working in concert as a team
or are the two functions
at odds with each other?**

Many a salesperson has been able to take advantage of a customer because the Engineering and Purchasing functions were fighting each other. Salespeople have been known to work with Engineering to get the specifications written without Purchasing's knowledge. If this happens, Purchasing has little say in the selection of the supplier and, consequently, limited power to negotiate the best deal.

Engineering must continuously evaluate methods for cost reduction through value engineering techniques and design for producibility rules and standards. A constant review like the following is required:

- **Can a method improvement reduce cost?**

- **Are there any substitute materials or process changes?**

- **Can the supplier assist in the design?**

- **Do we need the component at all?**

- **What ideas do you have to make the item more usable?**

- **Are there any features on the item which are not needed?**

- **Do you ever have to rework the item?**

- **What do you think could be done to reduce the cost of the item?**

When negotiating with a supplier, it is most important that the supplier deals with the purchasing agent about cost, not an engineer. When a supplier deals with a function other than the buyer who has been trained in the cost area, costs are typically higher. If engineering involves itself in negotiations without a buyer, the result can cost the company thousands of dollars.

SUPPLIER QUALITY ENGINEER — An Interface

The position of Supplier Quality Engineer (SQE) has several critical duties. The most important is establishing a line of communication between the supplier and customer with regards to cost and quality. The SQE acts as an interface between the customer and the supplier in the effort to reduce cost, cost of quality, cost of inventory and cost of product on a continuous basis.

At the start of negotiating a quality program, we must clearly define what is expected and establish performance goals. We should clearly define what we want from the supplier in terms of conformance to requirements and in the establishment of cost goals.

Prior to a supplier interface, most of these activities were not covered by the SQE. This meant that there was little communication between the supplier and the company. The SQE must be an integrated part of the process who assist in improving the product and reducing cost.

RATING SUPPLIERS FOR CONTINUOUS IMPROVEMENT

We also suggest establishing a supplier rating system, or "report card," to monitor a supplier's quality and performance. It's easy to forget what happened eleven months ago, but it won't be difficult to remember if you have a record of when and where both positive and negative events occur. Not only is it important to have a record of what went wrong, it is equally important to have a record of what the supplier is doing well. Concentrating on a supplier's errors will often create an adversarial position. Adversaries do not often try to solve problems, but defend themselves by building barriers and then attacking the other side. If you also concentrate on what a supplier does well, you can cement a relationship which will help you make improvements with other suppliers. This practice builds a foundation (instead of a barrier) so that both sides can solve mutual problems. It is best to bring everything into the open because sometimes you may find that something you do is the cause of your supplier's errors.

When initiating a performance evaluation program, don't expect results for the first half year or longer. Management should be patient through this period of time. Many companies make the mistake of going from no supplier ratings to rating all of their suppliers. To develop a supplier rating system for your company, we have determined from the numerous seminars we give on this subject that it is best to start with a cross-functional team made up of people from the following areas:

- Purchasing.
- Quality.
- Design Engineering.
- Finance.

- Manufacturing.
- Material Planning.
- Marketing or Sales.
- Management Information Systems.

You may even ask for input from some of your key suppliers in developing the rating system. Whatever you choose, the next step is to select a key group of suppliers, perhaps 10 to 20, whom you will start rating. Meet with these suppliers' key people to thoroughly explain the rating system so that they can rate their own performance at the same time you do. If they don't understand your system or found it difficult to use, then it will not be effective. You should also avoid subjectivity in your rating system. This is the quickest way to get into an argument.

Once you have explained the system to the initial group of suppliers, you can begin rating them. We advise against rating suppliers without warning. It is an adversarial tactic and will get your rating system off on the wrong foot. The goal is to help improve suppliers, not to beat them up. After gaining some experience (approximately twelve months), you are then in a position to add more suppliers to the rating system.

Continue to evaluate a seller's performance while you are communicating problems to the seller. When a supplier finds that a buyer is consistently reacting to bad performance, that supplier will seek to improve. Once improvements are made, the buyer should also respond. A positive response encourages the supplier to maintain high standards. A well-planned evaluation program will help a supplier improve because his performance is under constant scrutiny. In addition, rating systems can identify suppliers who have already worked on cost reduction or value analysis.

TRAFFIC AND TRANSPORTATION

You will find that the cost of traffic and transportation typically runs from 2.7 to 4 percent of a product's cost. It is easier to control internal and external freight cost if they are not part of the supplier's price. Our objective is to break down cost into all its elements. Negotiation means looking at each of the elements and getting the best cost for each in order to obtain the lowest total cost. Many cost reduction programs that we have seen combine or hide the real cost of the product. Another area of confusion is FOB terms. FOB delivery or FOB origin does not mean the customer can't control the cost. It means that delivery and title pass from one party to another either at the origin (shipping point) or destination (your plant). We should always break out the freight cost as a separate item. Unfortunately, few freight analysts have any training in negotiation even though they handle a large percentage of the total product cost. We feel that they must be included on the negotiation team.

Recently, we were attending a clients's JIT team meeting. The Inventory Group was working in a number of different areas to reduce the cost of their products. A young buyer told the group that her suppliers ship product into the company without charging for freight. We pointed out that freight is never free. It is incorporated somewhere in the cost structure.

Companies are now negotiating for lower quantities of components and increased frequency of delivery. There are a number of ways to coordinate the consolidation of deliveries and shipments. You may elect a single consolidation point for a common carrier, send your trucks to a geographical area every day or take advantage of back-haul rates. Standardization of shipping containers can reduce costs and improve accuracy dramatically. Accuracy of count, by the way, is often a hidden cost included in the cost of the material. These efforts will reduce the total cost. Every time you accept a 2% AQL (Acceptable Quality Level), you're paying for

2 bad parts out of 100. To add insult to injury, you're also paying to have them shipped to you.

Many companies believe that it is difficult to negotiate if your supplier isn't geographically close. Certainly it would be convenient if your suppliers were all next door. We aren't saying that proximity is not a factor, but that it is a factor you can deal with. At the Apple Macintosh plant in Fremont, CA, for example, we were able to receive products transported by ship from the Orient, 100% on-time, all the time. At the Kawasaki plant, their experience was virtually the same. Deliveries from Japan were always on-time, 100% acceptable and in correct quantities. How? By bringing everybody involved—customs, suppliers, freight forwarders and customers—together to negotiate timely and frequent delivery.

QUALITY MANAGEMENT

Like Engineering, the Quality Management function plays an important part in the make-up of the final cost of the product. The cost of quality, as noted in our book, **SUPPLIER CERTIFICATION:** *Achieving Excellence* (PT Publications, Inc., Palm Beach Gardens, FL), is made up of costs associated with products or services that do not conform. What we are really paying for is the cost a supplier incurs to make our product over and over and over again. We believe that the role of the quality function is to be a catalyst which aids a company in establishing quality requirements which will satisfy customer requirements. Look for the quality function to provide you with an estimate of what percentage of the item cost is comprised of waste, scrap, rework, etc. In essence, this is the same as an estimate of your supplier's cost of quality. Knowing this figure will provide you with a basis for your negotiation and cost structure. This strategy, combined with a supplier certification program as discussed in our book, will help you to reduce or maintain your cost structure.

MANUFACTURING

With some very large contracts or agreements, it would probably be highly beneficial to get input from the manufacturing function. We should look to this group to help us evaluate a supplier's facility to determine whether it can produce our product to specifications. In addition, the manufacturing function can provide information on the labor content of the product.

We're sure by now that you have decided that each of the functions will provide a real value to the negotiation process when you seek out their assistance. Will you take the time to research each of these beneficial interfaces? In a recent client session on reducing the cost of products, one individual advanced the suggestion that his company change a supplier's process to reduce costs. The manufacturing person from his company was upset that his function wasn't asked for input.

"Who knows more about bills of material, routings, process sheets and alternative methods of producing a product than us?" he asked.

The answer, of course, is your own manufacturing people, so include them.

SALES AND MARKETING

The role of sales and marketing is to provide a forecast to the procurement group of what the customer actually requires. This means that there should be a conversion to a corporate mentality which encourages total communication between all participants in order to achieve a successful negotiation. In many instances, you will find that the sales force can learn a great deal about manufacturing and other disciplines which will aid them in their approach to customers. In order to attain a win/win relationship, all behavior within both companies must support the agreement's goals and visions.

As an example, let us tell you a story about a distributor who recently attended a session in JIT Negotiation that we were conducting. About a half-day into the program, he asked to talk to me at lunch about his ideas on how to satisfy his customers and bring them and the Original Equipment Manufacturers (OEMs) into a total partnership. He discovered that he could determine the total cost of his products by finding out the cost of quality and inventory carrying cost of his customers. Then, he said, he and his customers could look at areas of cost savings.

His goal was to supply his customers with one-stop shopping. Today, this company delivers components to the factory floors of numerous companies. They don't stop in receiving, inspection, storeroom or warehouse areas. The components go directly to the point of use where the supplier replenishes the bins. The distributor sends a monthly invoice which has eliminated all matching of invoices, receipts and inventory management for each item.

TECHNICAL GROUPS

All too often, the technical functions of a company do not utilize the services of the purchasing function. It is important to get early involvement of the specification group in the negotiation process. We must avoid putting a specific supplier's name on a specification or blueprint. Otherwise, it is almost impossible to gain a cost advantage since the supplier knows the job is already theirs. Only when all parties understand the process we have presented in this book will successful negotiation take place.

CONSULTANTS

We have found that using a specialist can often provide you with needed expertise that your company may not have on board. For example, a company that wishes to purchase an environmental control system may hire a specialist who knows how to establish requirements which meet federal standards.

Recently, we were contacted by a company that wanted to buy a Manufacturing Requirement Planning system. They contracted with us to provide them with the data requirements to manage their business. They prepared a Request for Proposal (RFP) from our initial work and then gathered responses which they evaluated to determine if their requirements were met. We were then called back to review their final selection. This company used outside services to provide expertise and guidance which they did not have.

SUMMARY

This chapter has presented you with an outline of the baseline requirements for each function of your company. We have tried to get across the importance of encouraging each and every person to be involved. We understand that, in many cases, egos can get in the way of people working together. But, it is time to cast aside the attitude that Purchasing or Engineering has all the answers. Asking for help provides an excellent start for opening up a company-wide discussion. You know how little children always ask the question "Why?" until they get an answer. Grown-ups, on the other hand, have all the answers and they just make statements. Maybe it's time to learn something from our earlier years before it's too late.

CHAPTER NINE

My mother told me this many years ago:

"If you have to think whether it's right or wrong, it's probably wrong."
— Mary Grieco

GETTING
TO AN AGREEMENT

The last step of the negotiation process is reaching an agreement or closing the deal. At all times in negotiation, try to create a total package. When discussing something that your opponent deems important, make sure you get to discuss something important to you. Likewise, make sure that concessions are beneficial to both parties.

Once you have reached agreement, monitor the seller's perform-ance. A supplier who consistently delivers on-time is entitled to payment per the terms of the agreement or other considerations. When it comes to paying supplier's invoices, many companies think of maximizing their cash flow, rather than living up to their side of the bargain. The companies that pay their bills on time often find it easier to get suppliers to comply with their requests. That's because one of the criteria that suppliers use to rate their customers is how quickly they pay.

A supplier who does not adhere to the delivery schedule as part of the agreement might find themselves with less business in the future. This is the message that you must convey to your suppliers. If they perform well, they will be treated well. If not, business and a partnership may be lost. On the other hand, you should be willing to work with each supplier when a problem does arise. Try to be flexible. Let the supplier know that consistency and quality pays off.

People and companies tend to respond in kind. Therefore, half of the responsibility for creating a win/win atmosphere is yours. Remember that the negotiations aren't over simply because you have signed an agreement. The contract still has to be fulfilled and if you have been less than cooperative in your dealings with the supplier, you may pay dearly when you need to change anything in the agreement.

One owner of a construction-related company told me an interesting story of just how dearly heavy-handed negotiators will pay. This owner has a philosophy which he calls "Creative Change Order Management." For every job he takes on, he is over 99 percent sure that it will require some type of specification change prior to the job being completed. In one particular job, the purchasing agent for his customer had beaten him down badly. When the owner signed the contract, it was at cost. There was *no profit* at all. But the owner said he knew his day would come to even the score.

Sure enough, the purchasing agent calls to make a specification change which requires that 400 different vents than those specified in the contract be installed. The owner laughed when he told me that his company was in the middle of the job and that his customer had no other choice than to use him because a change in construction companies would have resulted in delays, causing prohibitive increases in the cost of the building. He told the agent that he would call back after he checked out where he was in the job.

When the owner called back, he quoted $625 per vent due to the enormity of the change. There was silence on the other end. The owner wondered whether the purchasing agent had a heart attack. After the agent regained his voice, there was a heated negotiation in which they settled on $275 per vent. The owner said that the agent felt pretty good about getting a substantially lower price, but that he felt really good himself. His costs were only $22 per vent. What had been a no-profit job turned into a highly profitable one. The owner concluded by saying that if you beat him up unfairly at the beginning, you will pay dearly in the end.

COMPETITION

When a buyer and a supplier have a good relationship, both sides can work to increase profits and push costs down. Without that relationship, a supplier who is asked to reduce costs may be tempted to sacrifice quality. Let's say, for example, that your supplier could cut costs if it was able to update its production equipment. It might be to your advantage to arrange a loan so that the supplier is able to purchase more efficient machinery. Over the long run, costs would be reduced because quality had improved.

For example, one of our clients was working with a supplier on the development of a new product. The supplier came up with a very innovative design approach which would bring costs significantly below the design to cost goals. But, the supplier needed a new piece of equipment to manufacture one of the parts. This was difficult because the outlay would mean a sizable investment for this cash-constrained company. Our client proposed an agreement in which the supplier would sell the part at the higher design to cost price and that the order would be for 42,000 units, or ten months of forecasted usage. The difference between the design to cost price and the new price times 42,000 was the cost of the piece of equipment. After the original order of 42,000 units, the price would then return to the lower new price.

Our client also put the supplier in contact with their banker with whom they had discussed their innovative arrangement. The banker not only granted the loan for the new piece of equipment, but also helped the supplier restructure his debt on more favorable terms. Our client now has what it considers to be a true partnership with this supplier who has very innovative design skills. To show their appreciation of our client, the supplier conducted a value analysis on other products.

UTILIZING PARTNERS

Another negotiation tactic is to decrease the number of suppliers from which you purchase and only use partners. The following example shows what one company was able to accomplish by using this strategy.

A company in New Hampshire which makes furniture to house CAD/CAM systems, has a 60,000 square foot sheet metal manufacturing shop. They used to carry sixteen different gauges of sheet metal to make three grades of their furniture. We helped them establish a purchasing/redesign program which enabled them to reduce the number of gauges from sixteen to four and the number of stored sheets of sheet metal from 9,000 to 300. The program eliminated a whole warehouse.

The company was then able to use only two suppliers to ship the four sizes to them every day. The buyer negotiated the contract, price and agreement, but the program is set up so that the receiving person calls the supplier and tells him what and when to deliver. The buyer doesn't get involved until the contract needs to be renewed. It's all prearranged right down to the lowest level on the manufacturing floor. Since there is a built-in release mechanism for an order, the company is saving money on storage and procurement costs. The more automatic and the lower down the totem pole you can push the release decision, the less internal costs you will incur.

The closer to the point of use you can have quantities released, the better the control you have on inventory levels. The person using the material will not need to pad inventory with safety stock, large lot sizes or earlier than needed delivery dates once he has confidence in the supplier. These three circumstances most often occur when there is either a great distance in time, space or managerial level between the person using the material and the person releasing it.

This kind of agreement with your suppliers is only possible when you negotiate with suppliers who go through the steps on the following page.

ONE-STOP SHOPPING

You can broaden the concept of supplier relationships by thinking of purchases in terms of families, or one-stop shopping. Tradition-

| Deliver on-time. |
| Understand flexibility. |
| Produce a quality product. |
| Implement Statistical Process Control. |
| Have established a long-term partnership. |
| Participate in value analysis and cost reduction. |

ally, purchasing has conducted business one order at a time. The more items you can group together in negotiations, the better the chance for achieving a lower total cost. That means agreements of a longer duration between you and your supplier. One of the benefits of doing this is to gain significantly lower costs for the long-term. Short-term buying is not the way of the future. From the supplier's perspective, they are getting something they want very much and that is a long-term relationship. You can now both concentrate on managing the relationship, rather than placing or soliciting orders.

Peter Garcia, materials manager of ShareBase, a division of Teradata, recently followed this approach with sheet metal parts for the company's cabinet assembly. They used to buy various parts from different suppliers. By consolidating all the components with one supplier, Peter says that some parts went up in cost and some parts came down in cost. However, the total cost was significantly reduced.

In a long-term agreement, the cost structure can often be reduced significantly. If we are buying an item for $1 and supplier can reduce the cost by ten cents, then we should be willing to insure that the supplier's profit margin is higher. This will motivate the supplier to investigate further cost reductions which might cause us to change our specifications, manufacturing cycle or paperwork and handling processes. Suppliers will do the work for us and increase both their profits and ours at the same time.

It is important that we work with suppliers in the understanding of this equation:

Selling Price = Profit + Cost

Both our efforts need to be focused on reducing cost. If we are committed and our suppliers are motivated, then there is plenty of room to reduce the supplier's selling price and increase their profits by reducing cost as the example above showed.

DEADLINES AND DEADLOCKS

Forcing another party to reach an agreement is often the time when deadlocks occur. When establishing a deadline in order to reach an agreement, be sure that you don't let deadlines force you to act. Try to control the situation and remain cool under the pressure. If possible, try to avoid making any deadlines to begin with. Remember that all deadlines are negotiable.

If you are faced with a real deadline in which you want a supplier to perform before an agreement has been reached, you can agree to conclude the negotiations later. Make sure you do so in good faith and that you don't take advantage of the other party when the pressure is off.

Deadlocks occur when both parties dig in and won't budge. It's like trench warfare. You fight for weeks over a few yards of earth. Here are some ways to break a deadlock:

• **Summarize**	**Find out what both of you do agree upon.**
• **Ask questions**	**Open up the discussion again by asking what the other party wants without reacting emotionally yourself.**
• **Use outside criteria**	**Compare the process of the negotiations against objective criteria, so you don't become entrenched again.**
• **Postpone**	**Agree to disagree later. Put off difficult parts of the negotiations until another time.**
• **Take a break**	**A shorter variation of the above. Come back and negotiate when tempers have died down.**
• **Split the difference**	**This often allows both sides to save face.**
• **Change partners**	**Have other people on both sides conclude the negotiations.**

The majority of negotiations are completed in the last five minutes of the process. We can remember a negotiation with a large Taiwanese company which ran day and night for five days. By the third day, they had almost succeeded at wearing us down. But, our ploy at this point was to call a caucus and take off for that evening and part of the next day. The Taiwanese told us that if we didn't reach an agreement by Friday, they would start to negotiate with other parties.

At 11:30 a.m. on the next morning, we called the company and told them that we hadn't reached a consensus amongst ourselves and that we needed more time. We told them that we could meet again at 1:00 p.m. on Friday, the day we were leaving. They were very concerned, but we simply said that if there was no deal, so be it. Eventually, we met and made a deal.

GETTING OUT OF A DEAL

Here is a chance to use everything you have learned in this book about being creative. Getting out of a deal has to be a win/win situation as well. Think twice, however, before you enter into any agreement. It's harder to get out of them than to get into them, sort of like marriages.

People are often tempted to take shortcuts when they want to get out of a deal. A short cut today may cost you dearly in the future. The waiting rooms of companies are where stories are often told of how a company or individual operates. The short cut you take with one company may cause other companies to factor in additional dollars when they deal with you, just in case. By being honest and trusting with our suppliers, we can get rid of this JIC (Just-In-Case) attitude which often exists on both sides. There is a saying that says, "In God we trust. All others need to provide documentation." What that means is that trust has to be earned on both sides over time. So when you take an action, think about whether your actions are building trust or destroying trust.

CONCLUSION

Now you have knowledge of the win/win negotiation philosophy and the tools to put it into action. We think that you will find this style of negotiation to be the most fruitful because it helps both sides reach their goals and satisfy their needs. It's good psychology and it's good business sense. Negotiate for success!

GLOSSARY

ABC CLASSIFICATION-Stratification of Inventory items in decreasing order of annual dollar volume. This array is then split into three classes, called A, B, and C. Class A contains the items with the highest annual dollar volume and receives the most attention. The medium class B receives less attention, and class C, which contains the low dollar volume items, is controlled routinely.

ACKNOWLEDGEMENT-A communication by a supplier to advise a purchaser that a purchase order has been received. It usually implies acceptance of the order by the supplier.

ACTION MESSAGE-An output of an MRP system that identifies the need for and the type of action to be taken to correct a current or potential material coverage problem.

ACTIVE INVENTORY-Covers raw material, work-in-process, and finished products which will be used or sold within the budgeted period without extra cost or loss.

ACTUAL COSTS-Those labor and material costs which are charged to a job as it moves through the production process.

AGGREGATE FORECAST-An estimate of sales for some grouping of products; perhaps for all products produced by some manufacturing facility.

AGGREGATE INVENTORY-The sum of the inventory levels for individual items. For example, the aggregate finished goods inventory would be made up of one half the sum of all the lot sizes plus the sum of all of the safety stocks plus anticipated inventory plus transportation inventory.

ANNUALIZED CONTRACTS-A method of acquiring materials which helps ensure continuous supply of material, minimizes forward commitments, and provides the supplier with estimated future requirements.

ARRIVAL DATE-The date purchased material is due to arrive at the receiving site. Arrival date can be input; can be equal to the current due date; or can be calculated from ship date plus transit time. Synonym: expected receipt date.

ASSEMBLY-A group of subassemblies and/or parts which are put together. The total unit constitutes a major consolidation of the final product. An assembly may be an end item or a component of a higher level assembly. See: component, subassembly

AVAILABLE MATERIAL-A term usually interpreted to mean "material available for planning" and thus including not only the on hand inventory, but also inventory on order. Material "available to promise" would, of course, be only the material on hand which has not been assigned.

AVAILABLE INVENTORY-In a simple inventory system, this is the sum of one-half the lot sizes plus the reserve stock in formula calculations.

BACKLOG-All of the customer orders booked, i.e., received but not yet shipped. Sometimes referred to as "open orders."

BACKORDER-An unfilled customer order or commitment. It is an immediate (or past due) demand against an item whose inventory is insufficient to satisfy the demand.

BID-A price, whether for payment or acceptance. A quotation specifically given to a prospective purchaser upon their request, usually in competition with other suppliers.

BILL OF LADING (UNIFORM)-A carrier's contract and receipt for goods which it agrees to transport from one place to another and to deliver to a designated person or assigns for compensation and upon such conditions as are stated therein.

BILL OF MATERIAL-A listing of all the subassemblies, parts and raw materials that go into a parent assembly showing the quantity of each required to make an assembly. There are a variety of formats for bills of material, including Single Level bill of material, Indented bill of material. Modular (Planning), Costed bill of material, etc.

BLANKET ORDER-A long-term commitment to a supplier for material against which short-term releases will be generated to satisfy requirements.

BOOK INVENTORY-An accounting definition of inventory units or value obtained from perpetual inventory records rather than by actual count.

BREAK EVEN POINT-Point at which cost of goods sold equals sales.

BUDGET-The financial expression of objectives. The budget includes total cash flow income and outflow.

BUYER-An individual whose functions include supplier selection and development, negotiation, order placement, supplier follow-up, measurement and control of supplier perform-ance, value analysis, evaluation of new materials and processes, etc.

BUYER CODE-A code used to identify the purchasing person responsible for a given item and/or purchase order.

BUYER'S MARKET-A "buyer's market" is considered to exist when goods are readily available and when the economic forces of business tend to cause goods to be priced at the purchaser's estimate of value.

CANCELLATION CHARGES-A fee charged by a seller to cover the costs associated with a customer's cancellation of an order. If the seller has started any engineering work, pur-chased raw materials, or started any manufacturing opera-tions, these changes would be included in the cancellation charge.

CAPACITY-It is a separate concept from priority. The highest sustainable output rate which can be achieved with the current product specifications, product mix, work force, plant and equipment.

CARRYING COST-The cost of carrying inventory is usually expressed as a percent. It represents the cost of capital invested, and costs of maintaining the inventory such as, taxes, and insurance, obsolescence, spoilage, and space occupied. Such costs vary from 35% or more annually, depending on type of industry.

CHANGE ORDER-A formal notification that a purchase order or shop order has changed.

COMMODITY BUYING-Grouping like parts or materials under one grouping. It may be used to control buyer's items.

COMPETITIVE BIDDING-The offer of estimates by firms or individuals competing for a contract, privilege, or right to supply specified services or merchandise.

COMPONENT-An inclusive term used to identify a raw material, ingredient, part or subassembly that goes into a higher level assembly, compound, or other item.

CONFIRMING ORDER- A purchase order issued to a supplier, listing the goods or services and terms of an order placed verbally, or otherwise, in advance of the issuance of the formal purchase document.

CONSIGNED STOCKS-Inventories which are in the possession of customers, dealers, agents, etc., but remain the property of the manufacturer by agreement.

CONTRACT-An agreement between two or more competent persons to perform a specific act or acts. A contract may be verbal or written. A purchase order, when accepted by a supplier, becomes a contract. Acceptance may be in writing or by performance.

CONTRACT DATE-The date when a contract is accepted by all parties.

CORRELATION-The relationship between two sets of numbers, such as between two quantities such that when one changes, the other is likely to make a corresponding change. If the changes are in the same direction, there is a positive correlation. When changes tend to go in opposite directions, there is negative correlation.

COST CENTER-The smallest segment of an organization for which costs are collected, such as the lathe department. The criteria in defining cost centers are that the cost be significant and the area of responsibility be clearly defined.

COST FACTORS-The units of input which represent costs to the manufacturing system, for example: labor hours, purchased material.

COST-PLUS-A pricing method whereby the purchaser agrees to pay the supplier an amount determined by the costs incurred by the supplier to produce the goods and/or services purchased plus a stated percentage or fixed sum.

COST REDUCTION-The act of lowering the cost of goods or services by identifying and eliminating non-value added cost/price or waste.

CURRENT PRICE-The price currently being paid.

DEBIT MEMO-Document used to authorize the shipment of rejected material back to the supplier and create a debit entry in accounts payable.

DELINQUENT ORDER-A line item on the customer open order which has an original schedule ship date prior to the current date.

DELIVERY CYCLE-The actual time from the receipt of the customer order to time of the shipment of the product.

DELIVERY SCHEDULE-The required or agreed time or rate of delivery of goods or services purchased for future period.

DEMAND-A need for a particular product or component. The demand could come from any number of sources, i.e., customer order, forecast, interplant, branch warehouse, service part, or to manufacturing the next higher level.

DEPENDENT DEMAND-Demand is considered dependent when it is directly related to or derived from the demand for other items or end products.

DEPRECIATION-An allocation of the original value of an asset against current income represent the declining value of the asset as a cost of that time period.

DETAILED SCHEDULING-The actual assignment of target starting and/or completion dates to operations or groups of operations to show when these must be done if the manufacturing order is to be completed on time. These dates are used in the dispatching operation.

DIRECT COSTS-Variable costs which can be directly attributed to a particular job or operation.

DIRECT SHIPMENT-The consignment of goods directly from the supplier to the buyer. Frequently used where a third party (distributor) acts as intermediary agent between supplier and buyer.

DISCOUNT-An allowance or deduction granted by the seller to the buyer, usually when certain stipulated conditions are met by the buyer, which reduces the cost of the goods purchased.

DISTRIBUTOR-A business that does not manufacture its own products but purchases and resells these products, usually maintaining an inventory of miscellaneous products.

DROP SHIPMENT-A distribution arrangement in which the seller serves as a selling agent by collecting orders but does not maintain inventory. The orders are sent to the manufacturer which ships directly to the customer.

DUE DATE-The date at which purchased material or production on order is due to be available for use.

DUTY-A tax levied by a government on the importation, exportation, or use and consumption of goods.

ECONOMIC ORDER QUANTITY (EOQ)-Determines the amount of product to be purchased or manufactured at one time in order to minimize the total cost involved, including the ordering costs (set-up of machines, writing orders, checking receipts, etc.) and carrying costs (costs of capital invested, insurance, taxes, space, obsolescence, and spoilage).

ENGINEERING CHANGE-A revision to a parts list, bill of materials or drawings. Changes are usually identified by a control number and are made for "Safety," "Cost Reduction," or "Functionality" reasons. In order to effectively implement engineering changes, all affected functions such as Materials, Quality, Assurance, Assembly Engineering, etc., should review and agree to the changes.

ENGINEERING DRAWINGS-A blueprint that visually presents the dimensional characteristics of a part or assembly at some stage of manufacture.

ESCALATION-An amount or percent by which a contract price may be adjusted if specified contingencies occur, such as changes in supplier's raw material or labor costs.

EXPEDITING-The "Prioritization" or "Tracing" of production or purchase orders which are needed in less than the normal lead time.

EXPEDITOR-A person whose primary duties are expediting.

EXPLOSION-An extension of a bill of material into the total of each of the components required to manufacture a given quantity of upper-level assembly or sub-assembly.

FABRICATION-A term used to distinguish manufacturing operations from assembly operations.

FINISHED GOODS INVENTORIES-Inventories on which all manufacturing operations, including final test, have been completed. These may be either finished parts, like replacement parts, or finished products which have been authorized for transfer to the finished stock account. These products are now available for shipment to the customer either as end items or replacement parts.

FOB (FREE ON BOARD)-The term means the seller is required to place the goods aboard the equipment of the transporting carrier without cost to the buyer. The term "F.O.B." must be qualified by a name of location, such as shipping point, destination, name of a city, mill, warehouse, etc. The stated F.O.B. point is usually the location where title to the goods passes from the seller to the buyer. The seller is liable for transportation charges and the risks of loss to the goods up to the point where title passes to the buyer.

FORECAST-A forecast is the extrapolation of the past into the future. It is an objective computation involving data as opposed to a prediction or subjective estimate incorporating management's anticipation of changes.

FUTURES-Contracts for sale and delivery of commodities at a future time, made with the intention that no commodity be delivered or received immediately.

GROSS REQUIREMENTS-The total of independent and dependent demand for a component or an assembly prior to the netting of inventory and scheduled receipts.

HANDLING COST-The cost involved in handling materials.

INACTIVE INVENTORY-Designates the stocks that are in excess of contemplated consumption within planning period. (Typically 12-18 months)

INDIRECT COSTS-Costs which are not directly incurred by a particular job or operation.

INDIRECT LABOR-Workers required to support production without being related to a specific product or assembly line.

INDIRECT MATERIALS-Materials which become part of the final product but are used in such small quantities that their cost is not applied directly to the product. Instead the cost becomes part of manufacturing supplies or overhead costs.

INVENTORY-Items which are in a stocking location or work-in-process location. Inventories usually consist of finished goods, work-in-process, purchased materials.

INVENTORY CONTROL-The activities and techniques of maintaining the stock of items at desired levels, whether they be raw materials, work-in-process, or finished goods.

INVENTORY INVESTMENT-The total cost of all inventory.

INVENTORY POLICY-A statement of philosophy which directs the management of inventory upon which procedures will be established.

INVENTORY SHRINKAGE-Losses resulting from scrap, deterioration, pilferage, etc.

INVENTORY TURNOVER-The number of times that the inventory dollar value is consumed by cost of goods sold during the year. The way to compute inventory turnover is to divide the cost of goods sold by the average inventory value.

INVENTORY USAGE-The amount of inventory used or consumed over a period of time.

INVENTORY VALUATION-The value of the inventory which can be calculated at either its cost or its market value. Because inventory value can change with time, some recognition must be taken of the age distribution of inventory. Therefore, the cost value of inventory, under accounting practice, is usually computed on a first-in-first-out (FIFO), last-in-first-out (LIFO) basis.

INVENTORY WRITE-OFF-A deduction of inventory dollars from the financial statement because the inventory is no longer saleable or because of shrinkage.

ISSUE CYCLE-The time required to complete the cycle of material issues. It includes generating a requisition, pulling the material from an inventory location and moving it to its destination.

ITEM-Any unique manufactured or purchased part or assembly, such as, finished product, assembly, sub-assembly, component, or raw material.

ITEM MASTER FILE-A computer file that contains identifying and descriptive data, control values and data on inventory status, requirements and planned orders. There is normally one record in this file for each stock keeping unit.

JUST-IN-TIME-A philosophy that promotes the manufacturing of the right product, in the right quantities, on time, at the lowest total cost to meet customer requirements.

KIT-The components of an assembly which have been pulled from stock and readied for movement to the assembly area.

KITTING-The process of removing components of an assembly from the stockroom and sending them to the assembly floor as a kit of parts.

LABOR PRODUCTIVITY-The rate of output of a worker or group of workers, per unit of time, compared to an established standard or rate of output.

LEAD TIME-A period of time required to perform an activity such as the procurement of materials and/or the production of products from manufacturing facility.

LOAD-This is the amount of scheduled work ahead of a manufacturing facility, usually expressed in terms of hours of work units or production.

LOT NUMBER-A unique identification assigned to a quantity of material to be procured or manufactured.

LOT SIZES-The amount of a particular item that is ordered from or produced by a manufacturing operation. Synonym: order quantity

MAKE-OR-BUY DECISION-The act of deciding whether to produce an item in-house or buy it from an outside supplier.

MAKE-TO-ORDER PRODUCT-The end item is finished after receipt of a customer order. Frequently long lead time components are forecast prior to the order arriving in order to reduce the delivery time to the customer. Where options or other sub-assemblies are stocked prior to customer orders arriving, the term "assemble-to-order" is frequently used.

MAKE-TO-STOCK PRODUCT-The end item is manufactured to and shipped from finished goods, "off the shelf."

MANUFACTURING LEAD TIME-The total time required to manufacture an item. Included here are order preparation time, queue time, set-up time, run time, move time, inspection, etc.

MANUFACTURING ORDER-A document or group of documents conveying authority for the manufacture of specified parts or products in specified quantities.

MANUFACTURING PROCESS-The series of activities performed upon material to convert it from raw or semifinished state to a state of further completion and of increased value.

MANUFACTURING RESOURCE PLANNING-A method for the effective planning of all the resources of a manufacturing company. Ideally, it addresses operational planning in units, financial planning in dollars, and has a simulation capability to answer "what if" questions. It is made up of a variety of functions, each linked together: Business Planning, Production Planning, Master Production Scheduling, Material Requirements Planning, Capacity Requirements Planning and the execution systems for capacity and priority. Outputs from these systems are integrated with financial reports such as the business plan, purchase commitment report, shipping budget, inventory projections in dollars, etc. Manufacturing resource planning is a direct outgrowth and extension of MRP (Material Requirements Planning). Often referred to as MRP II (2).

MARKET SHARE-The actual portion of available customer demand that a company achieves.

MASTER FILE-A main reference file of information such as bills of material or routing files.

MASTER PRODUCTION SCHEDULE (MPS)-It represents what the company plans to produce expressed in specific configurations, quantities, and dates.

MATERIAL-Any commodity used directly or indirectly in producing a product, raw materials, component parts, subassemblies, supplies, etc.

MATERIALS MANAGEMENT-A term to describe the grouping of management functions related to the complete cycle of material flow, from the purchase and internal control of production materials to the planning and control of work-in-process to warehousing, shipping and distribution of the finished product.

MOVE TIME-An allowance given on any order for the physical movement of items from one place to the next.

NEGOTIATION-The process by which a purchasing professional and a supplier agree to terms and conditions surrounding the purchase of an item.

NET CHANGE MRP-An approach in which the material requirements plan requires a change in requirements, open order or inventory status, or engineering usage. A partial explosion is made only for those parts affected by the change.

NET REQUIREMENTS-Requirements for a part or an assembly are derived as a result of netting gross requirements against inventory on hand and the scheduled receipts.

ON HAND-The balance shown in perpetual inventory records as being physically present at a stocking location.

ON ORDER-The stock on order is the quantity represented by the total of all outstanding replenishment orders. The on order balance increases when a new order is released, and it decreases when material is received to fill an order, or when an order is canceled.

OPEN ORDER-The quantity of a purchase order, sales order or factory order yet to be satisfied.

OPTION-A choice or feature offered to customers for customizing the end product. The customer must select from one of the available choices.

ORDER POINT-When the inventory level of an item (stock on hand plus on order) falls to or below the order point, action is taken to replenish the stock.

OVERHEAD-Costs incurred in the operation of a business which cannot be directly related to the individual products or services produced.

OVERHEAD PERCENTAGE-The percentage applied to a labor cost to calculate the overhead cost of performing work in that work center.

OVER-RUN-The quantity received from manufacturing or a supplier that is in excess of the quantity ordered.

OVERTIME-Work beyond normal established working hours which usually requires that a premium be paid to the workers.

PACKING SLIP-A document which itemizes in detail the contents of a particular package or shipment.

PARETO'S LAW-A concept developed by Pareto, an Italian economist, that simply says that a small percentage of a group account for the largest fraction of the cost.

PART-Refers to an item which is used as a component, an assembly or subassembly.

PART NUMBER-A number which serves to uniquely identify a component, product, or raw material.

PARTIAL ORDER-Any shipment received or shipped which is less than the amount ordered.

PAST DUE-An order that has not been completed on time.

PIECE PARTS-Consists of individual items in inventory at the entry level in manufacturing. For example, bolts and washers.

PLANNED ORDER-A suggested order quantity and due date created by MRP processing, when it encounters net requirements. Planned orders are created by the computer; exist only within the computer; and may be changed or deleted by the computer during subsequent MRP processing if conditions change.

PRE-EXPEDITING-The function of following up on open orders prior to the scheduled delivery date to ensure they will be delivered on time.

PREPAID-A term denoting that charges have been or are to be paid by the shipper.

PRICE PREVAILING AT THE DATE OF SHIPMENT-An agreement between the purchaser and the supplier that the price of the goods ordered will be based on the price on the day of shipment.

PRICE PROTECTION-An agreement by a supplier with a customer to grant the purchaser a price which the supplier established should the price increase prior to shipment.

PRICE SCHEDULE-The list of prices applying to varying quantities or types of goods.

PRIME COSTS-Direct costs of material and labor; does not include general sales and administrative costs.

PRIORITY-In a general sense, refers to the relative importance of jobs, i.e., which jobs should be worked on and when.

PROCEDURE MANUAL-A formal organization and indexing of a firm's policies and practices.

PROCEDURES-Definitions of approved methods of operation.

PROCESS SHEET-Detailed manufacturing instructions issued to the shop. The instructions may include speeds, feeds, tools, fixtures, machines, and sketches of set-ups and semi-finished dimensions. (i.e. routing)

PROCESS TIME-The time during which the material is being changed, whether it is a machining operation or a hand assembly.

PROCUREMENT LEAD TIME-The time required by the buyer to select a supplier, and to place and obtain a commitment for specific quantities of material at specified times.

PRODUCT-Any commodity produced for sale.

PRODUCT MIX-The combination of individual product types and the volume produced that make up the total production volume. Changes in the product mix can mean drastic changes in the manufacturing requirements for labor and material.

PRODUCT STRUCTURE-The way components go into a product during its manufacture. A typical product structure would show, for example, raw material being converted into fabricated components, components being put together to makes subassemblics, subassemblies going into assemblies, etc.

PRODUCTION CONTROL-The function of directing or regulating the movement of goods through the entire manufacturing cycle from the requisitioning of raw materials to the delivery of finished product.

PRODUCTION CYCLE-The lead time to produce product.

PRODUCTION MATERIAL-Any material used in the manufacturing process.

PRODUCTION RATES-The quantity of production usually expressed in units, hours. Expressed by a unit of time.

PRODUCTION REPORT-A formal, written statement giving information on the output of an organization for a specified period.

PRODUCTION SCHEDULE-A plan which authorizes the plant to manufacture a certain quantity of a specific item.

PROGRESS PAYMENTS-Payments arranged in connection with purchase transactions requiring period payments in advance of delivery.

PURCHASE ORDER-The purchaser's document used to formalize a purchase transaction with a supplier.

PURCHASE PART-A part purchased from a supplier.

PURCHASE PART VARIANCE-The difference in price between what was paid to the supplier and the standard cost of that item.

PURCHASE REQUISITION-A document conveying authority to the procurement department to purchase specified materials in specified quantities within a specified time.

PURCHASING AGENT-The person authorized by the company to purchase goods and services for the company.

PURCHASING CAPACITY-The act of buying capacity or machine time from a supplier.

PURCHASING LEAD TIME-The total lead time required to obtain a purchased item. Included are procurement lead time, supplier lead time, transportation time, receiving, inspection and put away time.

QUANTITY DISCOUNT-An allowance determined by the quantity or dollar value of a purchase.

QUANTITY PER- The quantity of a component to be used in the production of its parent. Quantity per is used when calculating the gross requirements for production.

QUEUE TIME-The amount of time a job waits at a work center before set-up or work is performed on the job. Queue time is one element of total manufacturing lead time.

QUOTATION-A statement of price, terms of sale, and description of goods or services offered by a supplier to a prospective purchaser; a bid. When given in response to an inquiry, it is usually considered an offer to sell.

QUOTATION TO EXPIRE DATE-The date at which time quotation price is no longer valid.

RECEIVING-This function includes the physical receipt of material; the inspection of the shipment for conformance with the purchase order (quantity and damage); identification and delivery to destination; and preparing receiving reports.

RECEIVING POINT-Location to which material is being shipped.

RECEIVING REPORT-A form used by the receiving function of a company to inform all departments of the receipt of goods purchased.

REJECTED INVENTORY-Inventory which does not meet quality requirements but has not yet been sent to rework, scrapped, or returned to a vendor.

REJECTION-The act of rejecting an item by the buyer's receiving inspection as not meeting the quality specification.

RELEASE-The authorization to produce or ship material which has already been ordered. (i.e. blanket order)

REPROMISE DATE-Revised delivery date obtained from the supplier which differs from the original contracts delivery date.

RESCHEDULING-The process of changing order or operation due dates, usually as a result of their being out of phase process or customer requirements.

RETURN TO SUPPLIER-Material that has been dispositioned, rejected by the buyer's inspection department and is awaiting shipment back to the supplier for repair or replacement.

ROUTING-A document showing the sequence of operations to be followed in a company environment.

RUN TIME-The actual time a job is on a machine or process in manufacturing

SAFETY STOCK-A quantity of stock planned to be in inventory to protect against fluctuations in demand and/or supply.

SEMI-FINISHED GOODS-Products which have been stored uncompleted awaiting final operations.

SERVICE PARTS-Parts used for the repair and/or maintenance of an assembled product.

SET-UP COST-The costs incurred with changing over a machine.

SET-UP TIME-The time measured from the last good part to the first good part produced off the next manufacturing run.

SHIPPING-Includes packaging, marking, weighing, routing, and loading materials for transportation from one location to another.

SHIPPING LEAD TIME-The number of working days normally required for goods in transit between a shipping and receiving point, plus acceptance time in days at the receiving point.

SHIPPING POINT-The location from which material is shipped.

SINGLE SOURCE-A single supplier is one particular source that you choose to buy from, although other suppliers exist.

SOLE SOURCE-A sole supplier is one that is unique; literally the only source.

SPECIFICATION-A detailed description of a material, an item, or a service.

SPLIT DELIVERY-A method by which a larger quantity is ordered but delivery is spread out over several dates.

SPLIT LOT-A manufacturing order quantity that has been divided into smaller quantities.

STANDARD COSTS-The normal expected cost of an operation, process, or product including labor, material, and overhead charges, computed on the basis of past performance costs, estimates, or work measurement.

STOCK-Stored products or service parts ready for use.

STOCK STATUS-A report showing the inventory quantity on hand.

SUBASSEMBLY-A component or assembly which is used at a higher level to make up another assembly.

SUPPLIER-A company or individual that supplies goods or services

SUPPLIER ALTERNATE -Other than the primary supplier. The alternate supplier may or may not supply a percentage of the items purchased, but is usually approved to supply the items.

SUPPLIER LEAD TIME-The time that normally elapses between the time an order is placed with the supplier and shipment of the material.

SUPPLIER MEASUREMENT-The act of measuring the supplier's performance to the contract. Measurements usually cover delivery, quality, and total cost.

SUPPLIER NUMBER-A numerical code used to identify a supplier from another supplier.

TERMS AND CONDITIONS-A general term used to describe all of the provisions and agreements of a contract.

UNIT OF MEASURE (PURCHASING)-The unit used to purchase an item. This may or may not be the same unit of measure used in the internal systems.

UNIT PRICE-A price associated with each individual unit of an inventory item.

USE AS IS-Material that has been dispositioned as unacceptable per the specifications, however, the material can be used within acceptable tolerance levels.

VALUE ANALYSIS-The systematic use of techniques which serve to identify required function, to establish a value for that function, and finally to provide that function at the lowest total cost.

VARIABLE COSTS-An operating cost that varies directly with production volume.

VARIANCE-1. The difference between the expected and the actual. 2. In statistics, the variance is a measure of dispersion of data.

VISUAL INSPECTION-A term generally used to indicate inspection performed without the aid of test instruments.

VOUCHER-A written instrument that bears witness to an act. Generally a voucher is an instrument showing services have been performed, or goods purchased, and authorizes payment to be made to the vendor.

WAIT TIME-The time that material would sit after being produced at an operation while it waits to be moved.

WARRANTY-An undertaking, either expressed or implied, that a certain fact regarding the subject matter of a contract is presently true or will be true. The word should be distinguished from "guarantee" which means a contract or promise by one person to answer for the performance of another.

WASTE-Anything other than the absolute minimum resources of material, machines and manpower required to add value to the product.

WORLD CLASS-Being the best at what you do. Product, Process, or Service.

WORK-IN-PROCESS-Product in various stages of completion throughout the plant including raw material that has been released for initial processing and completely processed material awaiting final inspection and acceptance as finished product or shipment to a customer.

YIELD-The ratio of usable material from a process compared to the manufacturing capacity plan.

Correct Answers to Self-Rating Negotiating Quiz in Chapter Five

1. — a
2. — b
3. — b
4. — c
5. — a
6. — d
7. — a
8. — a
9. — e
10. — a
11. — a
12. — b
13. — a
14. — a
15. — b
16. — a
17. — b
18. — a
19. — c
20. — d
21. — a
22. — e
23. — a
24. — c
25. — e

BIBLIOGRAPHY

You Can Negotiate Anything, Herb Cohen; Stuart Lyle, Secaucus, NJ.

The Secrets of Power Negotiating, Roger Dawson; Nightingale-Conant Corp., Chicago.

Negotiation, The MGI Management Inst., Harrison, NY.

Shaping Strategic Planning: frogs, dragons, bees and turkey tails, J. William Pfeiffer, Leonard D. Goodstein, Timothy M. Nolan; Scott, Foresman and Company, New York, NY.

Everything is Negotiable, Gavin Kennedy; Business Books Limited, London.

The Complete Negotiator, Gerard I. Nierenberg; Neirenberg & Zeif Publishers, New York.

Negotiate to Close, Gary Karrass; Simon & Schuster, Inc., New York, NY.

Getting to Yes, Roger Fisher and William Ury; Penguin Books, New York, NY.

MADE IN AMERICA: *The Total Business Concept*, Peter L. Grieco, Jr. and Michael W. Gozzo; PT Publications, Inc., Palm Beach Gardens, FL.

JUST-IN-TIME PURCHASING: *In Pursuit of Excellence*, Peter L. Grieco, Jr., Michael W. Gozzo and Jerry W. Claunch; PT Publications, Inc., Palm Beach Gardens, FL.

SUPPLIER CERTIFICATION: *Achieving Excellence*, Peter L. Grieco, Jr., Michael W. Gozzo and Jerry W. Claunch; PT Publications, Inc., Palm Beach Gardens, FL.

BEHIND BARS: *Bar Coding Principles and Applications*, Peter L. Grieco, Jr., Michael W. Gozzo and C.J. (Chip) Long; PT Publications, Inc., Palm Beach Gardens, FL.

SET-UP REDUCTION: *Saving Dollars with Common Sense*, Jerry W. Claunch and Philip D. Stang; PT Publications, Inc., Palm Beach Gardens, FL.

WORLD CLASS: *Measuring Its Achievement*, Peter L. Grieco, Jr.; PT Publications, Inc., Palm Beach Gardens, FL.

The 7 Habits of Highly Effective People, Stephen R. Cory; Fireside Book, Simon and Schuster, New York, NY.

Index

A

B

C

J

K

L

M